It's poetic, all of it; life is a chaotic paroxysm of unforced beauty, and you personify that. You're an aesthetic appreciation of that which spawns from the depths of the unknown - crashing waves of the divine upon the field of physicality before washing away as if you had never existed.

LOVE, SEX & PHILOSOPHY

Written by: Travis J.
Illustrations by: Henriette Kjeldal
Samson Vowles

I can almost hear myself now, what a voice I have. You can listen to yourself too, listen carefully. Receive the sound of your surrounding environment, the noise echoing an ancient source so alien to the modern world of humankind, we've forgotten what it's like to feel connected to it. Close your eyes, silence your mind as you hear and feel everything. It's pleasant; it's you.

You know, this is actually how I write about the woman I love who flows back from some future. I'm either deranged and poetically drivelling about a mysterious lover I've fooled myself into feeling within, or she's genuinely there already, and if I close my eyes and listen, I can not only hear her voice but I can discern her beauty as well.

The following pages are a collection of selected written pieces from over the years. This book does have some structure, a bit of flow, though it is primarily to be read for each piece.

If your optical jewels grace these letters my love, whoever and where ever you are, whether you happen to be more than one person or not - see this as proof that you were communicating with me through the ether.

CONTENTS

LOVE

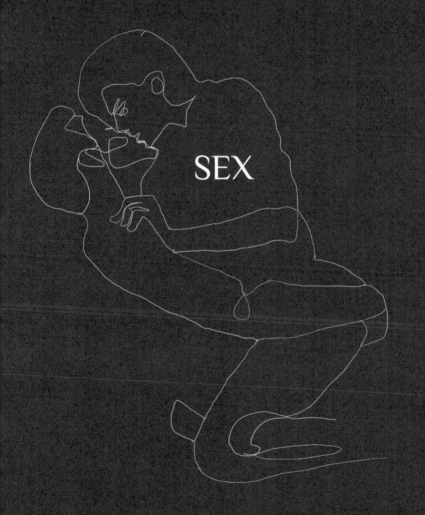

SEX

Throughout the recent years of my life, there has prevailed an ancient, enigmatic force within me that seems to be far beyond the age of time. I'm unsure exactly what it is; but it feels feminine, embracing, loving. I communicate with 'her' often, but such an engaging interest has contributed towards my desire for solitude. Consequently, if I'm not careful, depression often makes an appearance as I struggle to maintain myself in an ordinary world.

Though I am not defeated by this, not yet anyhow as I'm beginning to believe this force is somewhere out there, perhaps closer than I realise. And if I'm delusional so be it; but if I'm not, then I believe I have discovered something or someone unworldly among us.

Good sex begins long before you lie in bed with someone. It's founded in the eyes upon meeting and the laughter shared; this is foreplay. If there's any chemistry, if both feel the sacred energy radiating within their soul when they're together, then the physical play of love acts as a catalyst to expel it all through an orgasmic release.

Love & Sex

Speak to me. Show me who you are. Show me everything that lies hidden in the deepest and darkest chambers of your mind, so I know you're human; so I know I'm not alone - so I know there are still people in this world who know how to feel and question what this is all about. Your being and uniqueness teach me about who I am, and if I dismiss you, I neglect myself. Therefore, please, show me you're real, I won't laugh like them. I won't put you down for your embarrassments or judge your failures. The joke is on those who do as they will never receive the wonderful insight that comes from meeting the soul of a person; even if that means embracing their shadow.

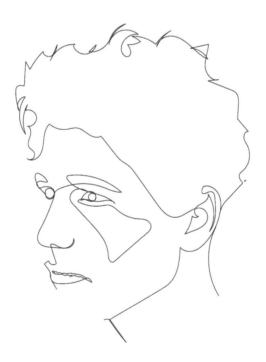

Communication in a relationship, whether that be with yourself or another, is like oxygen to the body; it's vital for a healthy connection. Sadly, many people fear the truth and respond immaturely upon unearthing it, so they suffocate it with ignorance or dishonesty. That creates a disturbance within relationships, something that respect alongside braveness could have resolved so long as the involved were open to confronting what is there. To continuously avoid what is real is to become a lie and therefore only attract as such. That is a self-destructive habit. How can you find what you deeply desire if you're unwilling to confront the truth without fear? I've experienced this many times throughout my life; some of the lovers I've danced with or the friends my heart has sailed aside in this ocean of life could not bear what was real. It was the vulnerability, the blaring light of who they are that frightened them.

Another issue with communication is how we articulate ourselves. We struggle to find the words. We're thin and shallow with our language because we haven't dared to expand our vocabulary. Within my generation, I find it amazing how repetitive people are with their speech. "I don't know, like, that's just how I am - you know?" Such a comment will only take you so far. I can't meet your soul and know your love if you cannot direct me to where you are. Everyone can say what they're feeling, but not everyone seems to be courageous enough. They opt for the myth, the surface level of expression handed by their culture and thus remain malnourished of connections that satisfy their soul.

She asked of me to undress her, to
know if she is beautiful; though
such a task is not as simple as
removing her clothes. To see her
naked, for what she really is - I
must know who awaits behind the
character she portrays for society. I
must not only hear but understand
her thoughts by a seashore,
midnight, embracing an ambience
of crashing waves with an
audience of stars. To meet her
demons, relive her fears, know her
history and feel the woman she's
become. Only then I am worthy
enough to judge.

What you show me, when you're not here for them, but instead in your most natural state is infinite. I can't get enough. I have a fascination with recognising your small quirks, the way your eyes look away as you capture a thought, how your feminine qualities embrace my masculinity. You are the woman the world needs, and I will support your journey either by your side or from afar. I only ask of you to appreciate yourself, to honour your gift for unravelling the unknown and perhaps take that conquering attitude you have radiating within and step into the person you know you can be. If you do that, then you will see what I see in you.

I do not write philosophy or poetry for the sake of attention. I write because there is a source within me I communicate with of which I cannot silence. Even closed-eyed, deeply asleep, it speaks; encouraging me to write these thoughts down at midnight, barely seeing but awake in another soulful state. Sometimes I wonder if it's just me, flowing through the ether from some future in another time, another world. Therefore, when I write of 'her,' when I vividly describe her presence without knowing or seeing who she is - it's because she stands beside me in that timeline. You can laugh at that, find it far-fetched but in my opinion, if that is your stance, then you haven't been paying attention to the bizarreness of existence. So much is possible. The expansiveness of love is proof of that.

I'd watch her from across the room like she was something entirely different from anything I've ever seen. But it was contradictory because she was everything. When the rays of sunlit air streamed on to her skin, and if I sat, looking at her for long enough - I could see a woman who had immortalised beauty. In my eyes, she never aged; I was never bored by what she presented to me naked or clothed, mentally or spiritually. I philosophically unwelcome this, but I must admit, I envy the man who is privileged to wake to her every day.

It's not always our decision who our soul falls for. Tell him or her your feelings; let them know you're madly in love with every quirk. Tell them that you find yourself within most of who they are, and can't help but to want to explore them entirely. Release those thoughts that knock on your heart, causing it to beat that little bit faster, and accept the consequences. If they don't feel the same, so be it - the freedom of expelling that loving energy is satisfying.

I don't know why we fear rejection so much, or why we enclose ourselves to our graves. The world could use a bit more honesty, love, and just raw humanness. Everyone is so stiff nowadays about their feelings.

Everything I've come to know, in every moment of joy and every memory of pain, letting go is the spirit of life. I've had the pleasure to meet wonderful people during this physical dream and fall in love with each one of their stories, their laughs and thoughts. However, as soon as my world collided with theirs, I knew we would someday depart, and continue our individual journey after learning so much from each other's universe. Such is life.

If you love someone, support them. It's not that you cling that little bit harder, rather, quite the contrary. You loosen your grip and allow your lovers and relationships to breathe for their growth and flow. Accept endings to value beginnings.

All of the other writers can write their poetry,
but I prefer to make love to the very body of that
literary art when I'm with her.

I don't quite know how to word this. Sometimes I wonder if most people are capable of understanding their emotions, if they can handle themselves appropriately when faced by that which will undo their fantasy as they feel the truth. I struggle very much to date, which is why when I fell for a beautiful soul, I submitted to the concept of marriage, which contradicted my philosophy. I later discovered who I had fallen for did not dance to the same song of love as myself, once everything was uncovered, and I found what I always do in all of my relationships.

People don't love themselves enough, which is understandable when the world is continually putting us down. So when someone comes along and says, "I absolutely adore the human you are. I love your slight gummy smile, your awkward laugh when you're nervous, your inability to look me in the eyes during a conversation because you do not believe in the beauty that I see. You're astonishing, astronomically gorgeous, and I want to experience all that you are," people immediately attach themselves. That decision eventually kills love and brings a world of suffering. Instead of solely appreciating the raw of that which underlies the ethereal connection - it's extracted, branded, demanded, culturalised, materialised in forms of gifts; you know - this is a con. I feel very alone when it comes to emotional maturity at this age.

I hope you succeed. I hope you find all the treasure you need to see yourself happy. I think of you to be someone special; ancient cosmic energy bottled inside the body of a transient organic instrument that plays the sweetest melodies. To have heard, felt, and danced to your song in a universe as vast as the human imagination was a privilege. You don't even know that I write this of you, but it is of my heart that I must confess the love I have for your existence. If you happen to read these fumbling words of a man whose voice weakened by your departure, know you're capable of anything you put your mind to. As of now, there is another source of energy that calls for me, somewhere, somehow - I sense her novelty and beauty, and I must go. Farewell.

I run my hand along her body. Her mind is deep. Treasure after treasure of wondrous, creative and intellectual thoughts lay hidden in sacred parts of her ocean. The world needs to see them; sometimes she reveals them to me in the moonlight. The truth is I've fallen in love, but I cannot swim. I am in the complete guidance of her mental waves and where they will guide me I do not know. An explorer lost in their love for searching - I have found my other; yet I do not see her.

There is immense depth to her soul. She carries meaning; I see it riddled upon her gooseflesh skin as my lips press upon her neck. I always try to read the cryptic messages that lay naked, but her body is too sacred for my eyes to translate.

For the most part, when we love - there is a recognition of a familiar warmth within the source. I know this because I feel it in her. But what exactly is this flame of comfort, and why do we experience it, let alone sense it within the presence of another? I have a theory that love is an ancient memory rather than just a drive or feeling. But to understand my thoughts, we must change our perception of ourselves and humanity, and consider the possibility of a collective mind stored outside the individual body of time-restricted creatures. There is, of course, the biological memory that passes through the genetic coding of your body in coherence with the tools of nature which forms your entire organic system each second. That remembrance allows you to beat your heart, duplicate your cells and sense the breeze touching your skin.

However, do we unknowingly receive information from a collective unconscious bank of all emotional happenings humans have experienced - consequently providing people of today with an insight we define as empathy? We naturally recognise what it's like to be defeated, to be violent, to be subjected to mistreatment and the creator of abusive environments because we are one organism growing through many lives. And our motive as such may be concerning the knowledge of what we are for the betterment of ourselves. So love is the recognition of an ancient event, source, fire flowing back from a previous life and into the eyes of your beloved. I sense in her what my ancestors felt when they first fell in love with the stars.

Sex isn't just sex, such as the heterosexual act of stripping down naked and inserting a penis into a vagina, repeatedly thrusting over the average duration of 3-7 minutes. That is an attempt to take away its real power. Rather, sex is the art of two complex beings coming together to express all the physical and non-physical about themselves as they become connected as one. It's an empowerment, a revelation that visually displays the embodiment of love. Love is painted to be seen on the bodies of humans engaging in a clearly godly experience. Take, for example, the ability to unify two people and produce another being as a result; that is what an omnipotent creator does.

Sex is also a form of language. During copulation, we communicate to one another on a level that words cannot reach, therefore, obtaining a more in-depth understanding of the person you are having intercourse with. We express ourselves by the movement of our body, the feelings that become present and fill up the atmosphere of our environment, the deep inter-connecting trance that arises by two minds and their physical selves unifying; these are ways of communicating information about oneself that words cannot convey. So it is clear why people who wish to take away your humanness to behave more like a programmed machine slaving away for the system will target sex and try to disempower the miraculous divinity of it. Be conscious of this. The disempowerment is evident in the influential culture displayed through mainstream media that resulted in a deduction of self-developed gentlemen along with self-aware women and concluded with 'booty calls' and 'Netflix and chill.' The body is an instrument. I'm not voicing against enjoying the symphonies heard when having your physical self played, but there is a significant difference between a classic Beethoven session of love and that of a 'one-hit-wonder.'

If you fall for a woman of knowledge, you should care to read her story. Just surface-level interactions will not suffice; loving only the cover of her book will lead you nowhere. It's her words that you must feel. To not only kiss her skin but to run your fingers along with each sentence of her beautiful mind. If you can do that, and are truthful with your words - then she'll know you're worthy of being a part of her next chapter.

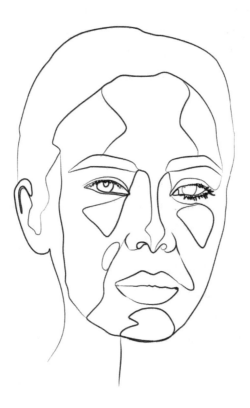

You see yourself fragile, afraid to love, so
you act tough and repress your emotions.
But what you deem weak I think to be
powerful; it's who you really are after all -
and to fear your own love externalised in
who you've fallen for is a limitation on
yourself. Yes, that means they will have a
part of you, and you'll be subjected to the
possibility of rejection and heartbreak;
perhaps worse if you fall for someone
who needs love the most.

However, I considerably disagree with your
decision to avoid love. You are human, and a
gorgeous one too with such a wonderful aura
that it is a shame you're too frightened to colour
this world as the sensitive and caring person I
know you to be. Understandably, you've
suffered before by this brave act of giving
yourself to another - but you were young and
full of naivety towards the truth that nothing
lasts. You've grown since then; you're aware
now. We need more people like you, so please
be you; express your heart, mind, soul and
energy without fear. Love again - the world
needs it.

I want to create a whole new word to describe you. Beautiful doesn't cut it; poets throw about that word too often and have overused its worth, and you're not someone to be used. I want to capture your essence with novelty, linguistically touch your heart and translate your meaning for the world to know how you make me feel. If I can do that, perhaps you will notice me. Not the me you see in the flesh, cultured and groomed - but that which I am when society isn't looking. I would tell you this often, yet I know you wouldn't believe me if I did - you have the soul of a phoenix. I'm a writer, it's written all over your body; the hardships, your history, your defeats and breakdowns, I can read it all when my eyes grace your presence. But my god, the power and resilience within you is inspiring. You're a word I'm yet to create, a rendition of nature's elegance flowering the streets with your spirit. I haven't even met you yet, not wholly anyhow as you still hide parts of yourself from me, though this I offer you, my love and energy to the woman I am bound to meet.

I don't think I've ever experienced a force as empowering as it is devastating than the love of a woman who knows herself.

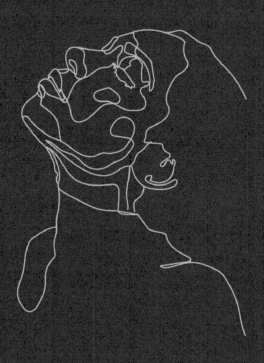

Where I sit from you
isn't that far when I have
these words to write
about you. I know you
feel me within each of
these symbols; my body
encapsulated for your
soul to touch as I enter
the gateway of your
eyes. Time is irrelevant
here; we're immaterial,
intangible - unbounded
by universal laws. Such
is love.

Expanding within lovers is an unspeakable universe. I don't know if you've ever experienced it, if you've felt the warmth of a million supernovas exploding every time you kiss or undress your lover - but it's real, whatever 'real' means. And to lay naked together or engage in an ethereal connection known as sex is to embody the definition of love and make it visible upon your skin. It's the purest form of art as your body is the canvas and your soul is the artist; but it requires you to be raw and to present yourself wholly, for who and what you are. That deters people, as we fear ourselves and vulnerability. Sex, therefore, becomes unappreciated and misunderstood, so it takes on a shallow form lacking meaning and beauty. As a cause, not many people understand each other or themselves; they would even struggle to detail the person their intimate partner is, yet they've met them outside of ordinary means.

Aside from the current desensitised culture that lacks appreciation for the body and mind - I think our inability to expose our humanness has impacted our sexual pleasure. We don't like to feel what we are, so how can we truly sense the touch of another if we're caught within thoughts rather than the felt-experience at hand?

Because It's magical to fall in love with someone who has just as much passion as you do for exploring the ins and outs of this mighty universe, and to be absolutely present with them. Not to speak strictly of an intimate partner, but to meet another mind you adore who's willing to venture into the most outlandish areas intellectually without fear is satisfying.

I have never found myself to be attracted to another human primarily by their physique. I am about the mind, the soul and their energy. I think physical intimacy is overrated, and people overlook the charm and pleasure in connecting with someone on a level untouchable. That is not to speak poorly of sex, rather, I am highlighting another layer of intimacy which seems to be lacking in most conversations, understandings and expressions of what it means to make love. A way of undressing another human and appreciating a nakedness that doesn't age yet possesses infinite growth. Meet a person at such a place, in such a divine state as your bodies interact in a play of love, and you will experience the very meaning of ecstasy. In that, I believe there to be an empowerment and respect for each other; something usually not found just within the act of intercourse and thus within the current culture of sex.

I could forever write about you. You compel me to. I'm not satisfied by simply running my hands along your body and kissing your edges; for I uncontrollably feel drawn to capture you in all ways possible. There are other women in my life, and gorgeous as they are - I always see you wherever I go. How can one man be so fortunate to encounter your angelic presence in a universe as vast as my love for you? Yet in my dreams is where you sleep.

Falling out of love, if you even want to call it that -
isn't something to fear or avoid. If you feel a
disconnection with your lover or lovers, and there is
no possibility to resolve this tear, then acknowledge
and accept what is natural; that everything ends.
Although, the irony is that we don't really have any
of this at all, not truly anyhow. Everything is
slipping through our fingers the moment we go to
grab it; that's how it works here. So, if you find
yourself approaching the unknown of what life will
be like without them, and you can sense the
inevitable heartache, understand you never had
them.

At the core of the human experience is a solo
journey, one that will become most apparent upon
death, which you will traverse alone.

Knowledge is her power; she isn't set on the attractions that lure most of her peers, her mind wanders elsewhere. She travels dimensions of imaginative thought I cannot begin to comprehend but only marvel in admiration of her existence. Like a star I guess, similar to the one I stare at this very moment alone in my tent in nature, as a man nakedly baring all in his writings on Christmas night. But be not mistaken, I write this of you, my dear. You, the brilliantly gifted soul who reads this, I see your body in space - illuminating the darkness with your light. I notice you, and you are not alone. And to prove that, I will offer everything that I am across all realms that structure the entirety of a man's physical and non-physical body to reflect your appearance in my appreciation for the interest in the sacred knowledge you thirst. In other words, where you metaphysically journey - I travel too, and together we can unravel the deepest mysteries of our exquisite universe.

Meet her by the shoreline of two worlds. Depart
with your body but present your soul upon contact.
Do not look away. Don't hesitate in fear of what
could be met. Steady now, breathe with each wave;
and if they swallow you whole then do not fret, let
them engulf your existence as you will not drown.
Love creates universes, and what an abundance of
possibility awaits if you give love a chance. You
believe it has failed you before, I know. Rejection or
loss has prevented you from returning here, but
those experiences are what brought you to this
moment. Everything has led to now. Steady, what
wakes you every morning is found within the canvas
of her eyes. She sees you. Not your ego, she reflects
the image of what you are when her eyes embrace
yours. She paints your potential, as you do for her.
If only you understood the connection you share.

Sex is like undressing the cosmic clothing of physicality and engaging with the raw essence of the universal energy. It's an act of empowerment - where you bridge a connection to elevate minds into a realm where they transcend ordinary interaction and into a dimension beyond linguistic description.

What is before me is no demon, perhaps a witch, but nothing to fear. She is not something separate from my being, no stranger to my history; she is who I think to be an expression of my feminine energy. I'm an empathetical man, a person who does not shy away from receiving the emotions of others, nor my own, for I communicate with this side of myself often, usually alone - and preferably in nature. There is profound understanding to unearth for the benefit of my masculinity discovered within the presence of her. If one is ignored, both suffer. If women do not bother to understand men, or if men do not allow themselves to be emotionally receiving - then we will continue to have the turmoil that exists today within our society and culture.

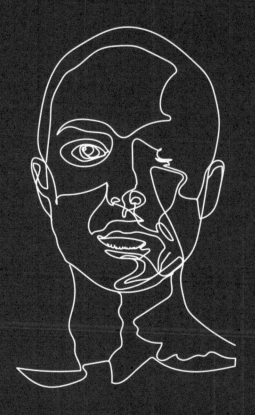

You don't need me, know this. There's
nothing to give you, nothing truly anyhow.
And if I'm not to be with you - remember
that all you require is yourself. Realise
this before entering a relationship; for if
you do meet another and discover a
connection without this understanding -
you will attach yourself and rely on what
your partner gives you. That will poison
not only the relationship but yourself as
well. Their thoughts will become your
thoughts; they'll seize control of your
energy as your very being becomes theirs
to manipulate - you'll internally be
destroyed. I see this too often, people
depending on someone else because they
think they're in love. They're infatuated
with the idea, the image, the outside
judgement, what movies depict as
happiness and necessary needs in
relationships. You know what love is to
me? It's the fact that as you're with him, I
wish nothing but for the universe to give
you everything you deserve because
you're worthy of it all. I'm sorry I couldn't
be the man you wanted, but know you
already are the person you need.

There's this woman who knows of me. She thinks I do not see her, though I cannot take my eyes off her. She comes here every night to read my poetry, not knowing she's the very inspiration of my words. It's that really uncanny and comical vibe; you know what I'm talking about? Where she probably thinks I'm in love with some mysterious woman whose beauty rivals a goddess, and as she reads she envies this person, not realising it's her wonder that fills me up with such madness that I happen to expel all of it within these symbols. Like, her eyes are consuming these words right now; it's beyond me.

There was just something magical about her. She roamed this world exuding love to everyone that crossed her path. She belonged to no one, no culture, no society, no nation, no religion, no race. She was a free spirit, and I think that's why I loved her.

After some time, you somewhat forget your previous partner; or better yet, place them somewhere within the depths of your mind. Even though what you both shared was once real, was so alive with passion - it now lies dead like a stillborn universe. Your lover becomes nothing but a memory, what a joke.

I still see her, as beautiful as I can remember her complexion. And oddly enough, her laugh haunts me; it was my favourite part about our coming together - the humour. I don't believe a day went by where we didn't lose ourselves in a fit of laughter. But whatever, I know she's happy, and that's enough for me to progress forward. I'm also well aware there's another galaxy I'm bound to collide with anytime soon, possibly multiple. For this is the thing, the chaos about love; it's unpredictable, and surrendering to its force is the only sane response.

You may never meet him or her. You may never taste the lips of a lover, as your heart is left unacknowledged. It's possible you will traverse this world alone until your dying days; your beauty never to be captured in the eyes of another, as your footprint as a human in the 21st-century is but a lonely one. You will not be forgotten, as you were never noticed. Your existence is a meteorite, out of this world you came here but do not belong here. Never will you attain your deepest wishes. You will know failure - ghosts of the person you could have been will haunt your every step. You will wonder why you're here, for what reason you should continue and if it's worth the effort. Madness will consume you; your bizarre dreams contain the colour you lost from the world as they express your weirdness. Nights will be favoured, the moonlight will evoke emotions buried deep within as music prevents them from becoming too destructive. All this and yet I have the nerve to ask of you to think of yourself lucky. That within what seems to be an endless universe, you have this time here, as this organic instrument with a story to tell, even if no one does listen. You are alive, somehow for not that long and my god that's enough to fall in love with yourself. You may as well be with it, through the highs and lows because it's not forever, but it's never to happen again. Love the surreal happening that you are.

If it were possible for governments to do, I think something as central to the human experience as love or sex would be made illegal.

We're so unaware of everything. This place is extraordinary; planets upon planets, galaxies upon galaxies, how do we begin to comprehend anything? Even our feelings are difficult to understand, for in every one of us rages a universe.

I've come to love you a lot; pretty much across the entire spectrum of what it means to be human. I can't say for certain why I do. I acknowledge the attraction of your physical complexities, your awkward smile and how you carry yourself which draws my attention, but there's something so familiar within you that fascinates me so much. You're empowering; I hope you realise that. I hope you meet someone who values the woman you are because to see you suffer again, due to the mind of a weak man, I know it'll cause you to internally collapse and become a dead star. I couldn't bear to see such a tragedy. Don't close the book of love after a lousy chapter, they're out there, seeking you.

She loves you, my friend. What else do you want? I know you, you're a good man, therefore be that and do something about it because her heart is not from this world. If you're sincere, which I've known you to be, then go ahead and spill it all. Confess everything. If it's the uncertainty that's preventing you, the fear of what will become of you if you're vulnerable, then you're mistaking yourself as anything but a human. We're naked as can be in an infinite space of nothingness with the light from stars exposing all that we are. There's no point to pretend. Call her; call out for what you know you love.

Like so many men, I am captivated by your
physicality. I know you receive such attention too,
although it's not the typical features that allure me.
It's your eyes that reveal a past, the tattooing on
your body which tells a story and the raw beauty
that like, pulsates from an aura which completely
engulfs me. This is, you know - no poetic piece to
translate immature feelings of a man charmed by a
woman; it's a confession to say I think you have to
be the most elegant person I've ever seen. And I
mean - that's just a fraction of you captured by
only my eyes. Wait until I write of your mind,
heart and soul.

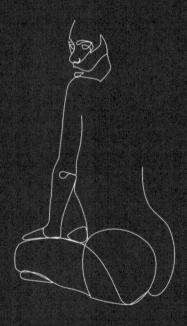

How do I say this, for I am yet to hear your voice. I see you; pervading my reality are puzzling messages and events that indicate your presence. Your energy is with me, some days and some nights. I've had my time here; faces are starting to take on a repeat as voices are beginning to sound the same, though what I hear from you if I listen closely enough to my heart is the unique sound of a soul I've fallen in love with throughout infinite lifetimes. However, I wonder if that love also flowed within my previous partners, that you continue to come on to me clothed differently, teaching me lessons I need for growth. I am bound to dance with many companions romantically, but ultimately - the song I dance to is a tune I've come to know as 'you.' So here's to you, all of you, and every aspect of your divinity I've so delightfully had the privilege to encounter throughout the many beautiful women who've revealed parts of myself I never thought existed. You are thrilling.

Without honesty, communication, love and the courage
to meet another's soul with your own - sex just feels
scripted; lacking any meaning or emotion.

Let me read you. You're afraid to seek out what your heart desires, for that move will expose you and make you vulnerable; so rather than express how you truly feel and engage with the minds you adore - you withdraw. You reach out for some mask that is popular in modern culture. You play your part, adopt the social norms and carry yourself in a manner to satisfy those you've outgrown. But how can you find the person who enlightens your day if you are not willing to be yourself? How will you greet those optical jewels that pierce your very soul like sunlight to eyes that have adopted the darkness for too long? He will not be within those places where you feel the need to fit in; she will not know you if you are unwilling to live truthfully - they will appear when you appear.

See, I know you; you have such a strong heart, but who you once loved mistreated it, and now you feel defeated. Therefore, it's now much easier to brush off potential lovers and only meet them halfway with flirtatious interactions as well as the rare one-night stand you regret than to involve yourself with such a connection again. Yet, I know there have been nights you long for a body to touch, a mind to explore and a hand to hold; I can read that as I write you here. Look, you will hurt again, most likely by the departure of another human, but you must realise life is fleeting your very body right now, and love is the most surreal experience. It would be a shame to watch you hide away from ever encountering it again.

I must state this while I have your attention before it's too late. If you're at the edge, standing before an enormous fall with a breeze flowing over you as lightning fills your veins, meaning, you're clouded by doubt in a storm of emotions - I urge for you not to abandon life but to look out beyond the horizon. There is much to be known; more of you to be discovered and a mystery awaiting the investment of your wondrous mind. It is not the end. The edge is your mind playing tricks. You limit yourself. You're physically out there, but internally you restrict your human experience to this island of thought, too afraid to wholeheartedly explore your passions you've come to this point in time - staring out into uncharted territory. Trust yourself, surrender to the fall of uncertainty and go forth.

You don't understand, she was not just a body that I made love to. She was a library of captivating stories and haunting truths that moved my soul. I wanted to read more; I wanted to know more about where she's been and where she's going. Each time her lips spoke about her past, she transformed before my eyes, like flipping pages through an endless book that had a beating heart. I don't know where she is now, but I will never forget what I learnt from her.

See, there is extraordinary beauty in a woman who is in love with the accumulation of knowledge. She is not bounded by the foolishness swelling in modern culture. She is freedom made visible, a delight to encounter and a rarity to behold. Any man who falls in love with her will have to meet her on levels of thought outside the ordinary; and those who do will grace the body of poetry. Believe me, I once did every waking day. But I was a boy then, and now the man I am today wishes I saw her for what she was.

Real intimacy, love, romance, soulful sex, mental stimulation, an ethereal connection with another person or multiple people - these are rare to discover. Most of us live out our days dreaming of these experiences, starved from the pleasures involved with finding someone so authentic, so natural and entirely there, we often surrender to either loneliness or decide to 'make do' with whoever we can. Not many people want to admit their relationship is only stable due to honouring some traditional beliefs and cultural expectations as a means to distract them from the truth that their partner isn't someone who completely embodies the qualities their heart and mind appreciates. They're too afraid of the lonesome reality that awaits and the opinions of others - they endure what I would I say is something that isn't even genuine.

I struggle to experience these rarities in another. I'm filled with integrity and cannot bury the lie that I am too unusual for the modern relationship and the apparent needs that follow. This will appear arrogant and hubris, I can foresee that interpretation even though there's no egotistical intention; this is just pure honesty - I feel so much more in tune with myself than the individuals I go on dates with. I presume that's the ramifications of relentless self-aware thought meditations and the effects of psychoanalysing oneself constantly. You become infinitely alive and united with your inner-self that you naturally fall distant from the majority and enter an entirely new world of intimacy. But that's quite unfortunate because there's not many people here to enjoy that level of bonding.

Sometimes, contrary to our nature, we'd go out and just enjoy the atmosphere of all the fascinating people out there. Unusual faces, mysterious disguises, engaging characters - society is teeming with diversity. Everyone has a story; it's written within the way they move, how they act and clothe themselves. And as two introverted empaths, we'd have an unbelievable amount of fun trying to read the stories of all these people bursting with colour. Most importantly, however, we bonded over the fact that we were writing our own as we looked for any hidden meaning that foretold the coming of our relationship within previous chapters.

Though, one day she left, which passed so quickly; she changed as we all do. And the irony is that I began to perceive her as one of those strangers. I guess this was life expressing its humour once again, as existence, including yourself - is far too complicated for us to take it too seriously; let alone attempt to obtain some form of control over it.

I'm a difficult person to love. I'm reserved,
I don't ask for nor give much. That has
cost me friendships and intimate partners.
My favourite surroundings involve
immense solitude; a lake or a mountain
where it's only my soul and the
atmosphere of the wilderness.

You wouldn't think she's human if you
met her. She possesses attributes and
qualities that vibrate on a whole other
frequency. Some think she's a goddess,
most think she's a witch. Me, however,
I just think she's real. She's truth, no
matter the cost; and I personally find
that to be very beautiful. Just soulful,
you know? Natural, deep, profound,
uncorrupted by society. It's why I love
her so much. I mean, who can blame a
man to fall effortlessly for a woman
that carries the essence, the pith, the
substance, the mystery of creation, of
what makes life so rich and authentic?
And she will, hopefully - one day carry
everything I am and in return create an
expanding universe bottled up inside a
living, breathing, growing organism
that I can call my child.

To my yet to be born child, one day I'll tell you about
the stars I would visit when I fell in love with your
mother. The whole cosmos knew her name and story
by the time I journeyed back to Earth. So fascinated
by her existence, they gifted you.

I think part of the meaning of falling in love with someone is that you create a universe. A universe containing shared memories, experiences, thoughts, visions, desires, hopes and dreams - in which it's existence is only real to the creators. So heartbreak, the loss of a loved one hurts so immensely for it is the collapse of an entire universe. It is the breakdown of a reality, causing the affected to feel lost, confused, and unaware of how to function without the other partner. You feel unsure of how to live within this new found environment of being alone that is always invaded by the transmission of memories of a past reality, a past universe that is slowing dying and fading out. Therefore, the only healthy response to this situation is simply to love again.

Loving someone is also like dancing to a song. When you love someone, let them know; say, "you are so divine, I cannot help but want to take your hand and experience this song together." But for some reason we shy away from love as one might shy away from a dance, for we are too worried about what may happen or what someone may think - and so we never truly get to express ourselves and experience its beautiful melodies. You miss an opportunity, a chance to connect with someone on such a level that you see through the illusory identity and witness the real self behind the act that is being portrayed. You interlock fingers and feel the way they move; two forms of energy dancing together to a drumbeat of vibrations in which existence is in a consistent state of. So a feeling of complete ecstasy occurs in which we recognise as love.

If this happens to you, just dance. Flow with the music, and let it take you on a voyage so wonderfully intrinsic - it can only be experienced and explored spontaneously. The cosmic energy expressed through the love of human beings is indescribable. Love will take you to places so beautiful that any attempt to use words to describe what you are feeling will do it no justice. It is a divine experience, a universal feeling of completion for you have found yourself in someone else; even death cannot silence it. If you're in love, I advise you to stop trying to dissect and question it for it is not something we can explain, we can only experience. So take one's hand and dance while the song is being played. However, when the song ends, and the dance is over - it is best to let go.

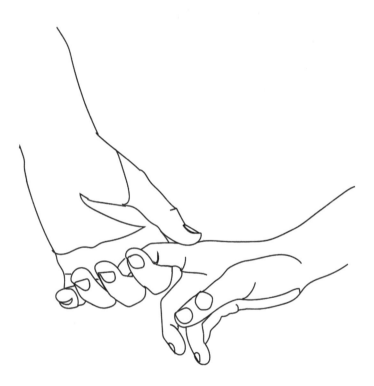

You don't know, they may be
thinking of you right now, late at
night, unable to sleep and yet you
believe yourself to be unworthy
of their love.

Tell me everything for you're not alone. Tell me your evenings of despair, desperation and suffering that keeps you awake all night and sleeping all day. Breakdown before me, man or woman and I'll fall with you. I'll meet your demons and listen to every word they say because I care to be human with you. I see you as myself, and I would appreciate the same love and support. If you cry, do so openly in my presence; you do not have to hide away from the fear of judgement - especially my fellow men who the world has misled by encouraging the suppression of our emotions, which is our humanness.

Listen, it's taken me quite some time to word this part, but I wish for you to know the truth. At the core of what I am, and in every lover you've embraced or individual you've hated - is the same source that fuels your existence. Why then, must we pretend that my experience is not fundamentally your experience and that if I hurt - you hurt? Such remembrance of this forgotten understanding would benefit not only ourselves but all of humankind as well.

I admire the spiritual, not the physical; in love with the philosophical, not the material - it is not how one presents themselves externally that attracts me, it is their internal-self that drives me mad with wonder.

That new popular item just doesn't cut it anymore. I want mountains and freedom, poetry and love. Give me a secluded forest in the heart of nature, sitting by a fire distant from the prying eyes of society and with a lover who shares a mind similar to mine. That is what I call living.

Of all the wonders in the universe, the untold knowledge, the hidden secrets that I thirst to discover and for all its beauty displayed within surreal galaxies as well as remarkable stars - it doesn't amount to what you contain nor the love I have for your existence. You fascinate me more than the cosmos. You actualise my dreams and embody the phenomenon in which my art has failed to depict. They'll laugh at me for this, although I do not care for what they think - but I haven't met you, or maybe I have. I feel your energy in my dreams. You don't physically show me much, yet from what I've seen your appearance is youthful - as your eyes are incredibly ancient. There's an intense gaze that haunts me even when I awaken and return to ordinary life; it inspired me to write this. I'll show it to you one day when we sit by a tree, mid-summer, surrounded by our books as we experience the physical presence of one another.

Why do I love you? It's simple; you're real. I've intimately danced with too many people who lie to themselves, therefore to encounter someone truthful with everything they are is compelling. So much so I dream of you, and that's love in my eyes.

There's an unspoken song within her; a heavenly melody that tells a story of a person made of magic. I'm charmed by her beauty. It has taken me months just to write this far; I've never been so in love. How blessed I must be that the creative lips of the goddess of nature have kissed my existence; that she has decided to take form as a human for me to fumble my words in awe at her magnificence. The fact that I can hold her hand in my dreams is enough to be filled with such delight. I understand, I know - I must seem to be out of my mind. But to lose my mind, I go into my senses, to feel her; and there she is undressed, timeless, radiantly naked and beyond everything I have just written.
This is love.

PHILOSOPHY

Bear with me, I want to see if I can briefly word most of my philosophy within this book. I think life is a mystery. I am for the spirit of science and the science of spirituality to unearth this enigmatic force present everywhere and in everyone, although I think it transcends the current means of understanding. It's more than language; egotistical chatter cannot grasp it wholly. I am not for the holy, the religious, the culture and all that blather permeating the brains of modern civilisation. I think the undoing of all those belief-systems is apparent by addressing what gives them structure and life, which is language. The state of meditation, when you silence the thinker and experience enlightenment as you interact with the mystery without words reveals that. The only problem is you can't speak about it when you return to reality as we don't have a medium to express it clearly; although love is fascinating.

Love transcends all, yet there aren't many words to express it. I dislike that about us. Humanity is a book. We write our story and what world we want; so it's bizarre we speak so much hate, so much war and conflict. However, nothing is as bizarre as you. You top the list. Your very being is just unfathomable. We delude ourselves into comprehending what we are by fitting into labels and clothing, but it's like filling a broken cup with an ocean of colour. Your ethereal essence just seeps through the cracks in your supposed identity. That has created a disconnection between us.

There is a lot of distrust and dishonesty, even in relationships that have existed for many years, people are still apprehensive about their partners. That is anxiety manifested, part of the root to our suffering as we lack the means and awareness to communicate and feel what's real. I believe we can do much better. I think if we value integrity by being courageous enough to embrace truth through disrobing the illusion of self, there'd be less disharmony and more love.

Look, there's something quite special I want to speak about; I want you to focus your attention on you. But to do this, I must be honest. I cannot give way to flowery language or conventional spiritual ideology if we are sincere about acknowledging the totality of what you are. There is no pretence here, only rawness sourcing from my intellect, and perhaps my soul. Follow these words at your discretion.

You exist in a realm that is neither here nor there. It is abstract and exhilarating, yet palpable and very dark. It will pull you across worlds of emotions, provide you with euphoria at times but strip you naked suddenly, exposing your weakness as it drags your broken body across the ocean floor. Elation is probable, suffering inevitable.

You will die too, very soon. No one fundamentally knows why we do, not truly anyways. Nor do we comprehend what became of the billions of humans who have already passed. Standing behind every human are the numerous ghosts of our ancestors. That will be you, possibly as soon as tomorrow.

Time is a funny concept. Here you are, but in actuality, you're not. For as soon as you read "here you are," you were already elsewhere. There is growth at play, a continuation to what seems to be forward yet I know it leads to nowhere but death. I'm sure that's a misunderstanding, just as most of our truths probably are.

On top of this, you are indefinable. All the words bouncing around in your mind or when you extract them through your vocal cords are empty as the wind. We've given them meaning, which in return has provided you with meaning. That is not to say they are powerless; language is the foundation of our reality. However, words are like code to a computer, which displays a picture for the observer to experience. I ask you though, what endures outside of that screen? Where does the observer sit? And is there a way to get there? That is the purpose of meditation. There is a real sense of self when in tune with everything as we unplug ourselves from the matrix. I've experienced as such; it's magnificent, and I felt I was more myself than I've ever been.

The part of me trying to make sense of what I am
is what distorts everything that I am.

I may physically be alone, but many souls from around the world accompany my pursuit of wonder and thirst for esoteric universal knowledge. In some way, behind the illusion, we are connected, whether we know it or not - to a collective source buried deep within history and underneath ordinary reality. I sense it at night, in my dreams and within the energy of someone I have never met, but upon their presence, I immediately feel as though our relationship dates back thousands of years ago.

Philosophy

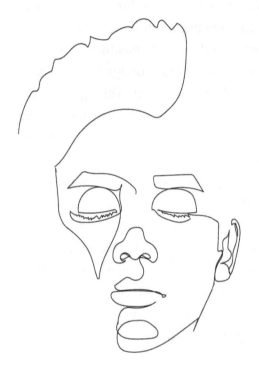

You and I are not for this. I know that because you possess the mind of an 'other,' you see things differently. You can feel the unspeakable within people. You can feel their true intentions and understand who they are without having to ask; which is why you often bypass the small talk and dive straight into the depths of empathetic conversations because emotions are not foreign to you. That makes you vulnerable but powerful. Although, the difficulty is within the fact that most are unwilling to meet you there - hence the eventual inward retreat that gives way to solitude and a deep admiration for nature. However, the pay-off is that you no longer have to lie to yourself, and when the time does come to meet another like you - you realise the worth within remaining true to yourself. It's sad to say, but do you know how many people just live an automatic existence as they follow a check-list, ticking off milestones and attainments without actually questioning if they want them?

Degree - check.
Wife/Husband - check.
Mortgage - check.
Kids - check.
Death.

Not to be pretentious, as if to say I have it all figured out - but I genuinely feel sorry for people who are culturally trapped by such a robotic perception.

I'm a young man - I know myself to be stupid at times. I haven't got much going for me, I never have, and I don't mind. I'm hardly involved with this world; I live in the background, working low-class jobs as I keep to myself in my quiet home. I feel out of place usually - nothing attracts me other than 'her' and magic. Philosophy, astronomy, love, poetry, conscious sex, nature, spirituality, this is where I'm at. My drugs are not your drugs. My highs are unlike yours. I don't drink, I don't party; I'm unorthodox and socially awkward when engaging with the dialect of my peers.

I have this unsettling feeling that I won't be here for long, perhaps because I was never meant to be. I've washed up from nowhere. However, I'm content with letting it all go, and in that, I've found peace. I'm unsure how many people can say that. I'm so aware of my insignificance that my anxiety is non-existent. I have nothing to worry about. I will come and go like the breeze of yesterday, which stimulates a sense of appreciation for today.

I have travelled to no greater place
than the depths of my own mind.

When you're ready, and by ready I mean you've reached a point of saying enough, I want to see and know more of myself along with this mighty universe than what they tell me - then something extraordinary happens. It's the empowering of a human mind choosing to reject the dehumanising programming that has limited and restricted the experience of what it means to exist. To feel more; to really get into the moment of this happening and be less involved with this fear inducing, anxiety encouraging game that has you mentally tearing yourself apart because you're tired of it all. You're tired of the social hierarchy, of having to play a character to fit in and be accepted.

I'd like to put forth this thought, and let you play with it. Imagine you stand at the edge of some faraway planet, looking upon crashing waves over a rocky cliff as you feel a breeze that flows through your hair. There, you are alone; the nearest soul is lightyears away. Where is Earth, you ask? Forget about her - you are beyond the Milky Way. You are way back in time. Way before the birth of any human to be, way before the formulation of our solar system, way before any supposed rotating gas cloud collapsed in on itself to source our galaxy - you are entirely alone in some ancient world. Imagine that. To be without history, without religion, without nationality, without culture, without race, without any notions or identity - you stand before the universe utterly free and absorbed by each wave that crashes beneath your feet as if to reflect your all-flowing existence. Now, in such a mystical place, in such a pure state of mind without the contamination of language, I ask of you to answer one question - who are you?

What I want for you to understand is who you are. To not fear your oddities; to know what you're capable of and that you are not obligated to live systematically. You don't have to maintain the charade. You can disagree with the beliefs of how one should live as you pursue an alternative path. Yes, you may be outcasted, forgotten or scrutinised. However, if where you travel does not impede the lives of others, and you're in tune with your intuition, then my friend you're doing just fine. That's unusual to hear, isn't it? That you are absolutely fine and have nothing to worry about fundamentally because stating this will reduce your anxiety, and you won't be as great of a participant in modern society. For what motivates us currently is our confusion that we are incomplete, and we need to be more. You need those new items of clothing, that new car, that new phone, that degree which gives you a well-paying job and the respect from your fellow peers. These are empty fulfilments when attained under this belief that you must have them to see yourself successful and happy. You cannot be either of those until you accept yourself whole, which is unlikely if you're raised in Western civilisation as we are taught from a young age that we are broken, and must become someone to be fixed.

If you feel you've intellectually and
soulfully outgrown a social
environment - detach yourself from it.
I know - you'll probably be judged
negatively by friends you've shared
plenty of history with; but if they
genuinely love you, and care for your
journey - then those who are worth
your energy will continue to support
you from afar. Surround yourself with
like-minded people and watch
yourself flourish.

You are entirely something different from what they planned for you to be. The grades were there, the intelligence and capability, but of what value are they if your heart existed elsewhere? You never did belong with them, the suits - you're too wild for this tedious system. I see that within your smile; it's liberating to observe. You have those moments, don't you? Time slows, the people around you appear less real and more like characters in a movie. Even in the most sociable environments, you find yourself watching, considering the meaning to all of this like interpreting a dream after waking up from a long sleep. Yes, you enjoy the moments of just being, especially when everything becomes too much. But deep-thought, investing your mind into the hidden crevices of life that contain untouched knowledge is what attracts you the most. You're like a witch, a wizard, a sorcerer of a kind imbued with a thirst for the magic which underlies existence. I like that; it's comforting for me to know there is another who is like me.

Take the thought that you will never be great. That you will never be known and the ambitions you have as well as your dreams will forever remain as such. You will live the most mediocre life, only to have served a system that allowed you to get by and live a 'plain' existence. We've created a culture to see that as unfavourable, and I am someone who has repeatedly encouraged individuals to strive for greatness. However, as an alternative perspective, consider the beauty that entails the lives of those who die cherishing the simple pleasures of life. Within the quiet man lives a world of serenity; an understanding expressed by those who watch crashing waves and wake early morning to capture the sunrise. I don't exactly know what amount of worldly success can match the fulfilment experienced when appreciating the simple moments nature presents daily, and how you could not deem that to be a life well-lived.

We've been through so much, you and I. It's unreal how the world suddenly ends; one day you feel like you're in a place that will last forever, the next moment you've changed and that place is now a memory. There were people just like you and me hundreds and thousands of years ago that were young and felt eternal. Now their bodies have decomposed, their stories are forgotten. All they cared for and all that they were is now nothing. We will soon be just like them, as someone else will take our place in the sun as earth consumes our ageing bones. No one really understands how close they are to death. In a hundred years or less, everyone reading this tonight, including myself as the writer - will be dead.

I exist behind the world of words and images. And every time I want to show you myself, to express my essence, I have to leave where I am and become a word or image. Consequently, I'm never entirely captured. That is the joke of loneliness, the truth of our apparent situation that has us separated from one another in this realm. To reveal myself, I have to become something else; which perverts everything I am.

The more you pay attention,
the weirder it becomes.

Where I am cannot be said. I could give you my geographical location, you can find me on the physical plane, but I am elsewhere. My mind takes me to the edge of the universe as I stand naked, alone in my shower.

At the heart of this all, I don't believe we must do something. That is my central view. I will choose to live purposeful, excite my ambitions, and find meaning in my wildest dreams. However, deep within I see no difference between a person lying in the gutter of a grimy street and a person flying above in a jet plane. At the end of everything, we will meet the same wave that will wash away all that we thought real. So, how do we respond to such a perception?

In my opinion, and the reason I live with such a view - is that purpose provides a playful experience to my human existence, but I am always detached knowing it's a blanket to cover my reality which reduces my anxiety significantly. I know I can engage and proceed through uncertainty with a smile because I choose to believe living is fundamentally for pleasure, even though it can be twisted and painful. While it is wonderful to pursue what attracts your soul, know you are free to live outside human affairs with the rest of nature in the ecstasy of just being.

Rather than trying to be someone, just be, while you can. Being is more fulfilling than 'someoning.'

Wake up every morning, dress yourself in clothing you don't even want to wear, work a job you dislike as you don a mask to fit in with people you can't relate to - only to then return to a home that doesn't feel like a home and mindlessly scroll social media feeds that make you feel defeated. Meanwhile, you ignore the passion that rumbles deep within, you know - that itch you have to write a book, start a podcast, make some artwork or write a song which is shunned weekly, for your weekends are prioritised to kill off brain cells at some club or party you don't even want to be at; knowing that no one there cares one bit about what your soul has to say. Break that cycle, please.

Only the dead are free from what we enslave ourselves within. And what we confine ourselves to is not what I would call living; it's robotic, tedious, ugly and decaying. So the paradoxical conclusion drawn from such an observation is that the dead are more alive than what we, the ones with the beating hearts choose to be. Enslave ourselves to school grades, dull jobs and TV dinner nights, that is not what I define as alive - that is repeated suicide of one's soul. I don't mean of this to be rude, but more often than not - I'm genuinely unsure if I am talking to a person who can produce their own thoughts or a hollow body in which their soul died many years ago from mutiny led by cultural programming and systematic lifestyles.

Consider the thought that you will be forgotten in the coming days. That everything you've done, all the words you've said, places you've been, people you've encountered and lovers you've danced with will bet met with no remembrance by the future. You will live and die like a short-lived feeling, and your life will seem as if it had never existed. Flowers will grow, leaves will fall, and historical events will pass - you will not achieve anything deemed remarkable by the human race. How does that make you feel? It's not to evoke a sadness upon the realisation you may never be a renowned individual - that desire of status is worthless. Motives for social popularity is like concentrating your energy into building many mirrors in your bedroom as opposed to polishing just one. Rather, I'm making light of the most probable case which is that your existence in the human world is as much of an importance to the cosmic order as the lizards that play in your garden bed. Although, with that notion involves the idea that being so insignificant presents the possibility of freedom; of enjoyment. To be able to bask in the sunlight without the anxiety of what will happen tomorrow as you are free from purpose, design and creation.

You are neither tomorrow or yesterday - only now; and in that thought arises great self-empowerment on the fulfilment of life. The best works of art are the forgotten ones.

It is without a doubt that you were raised to fail. The system is not tolerable of outsiders. It is a machine. It feeds on the human spirit, gnawing at the man or woman's energy - it chews away the best years of your life. From the educational induction through schooling and straight into the workforce, you are here to serve. To serve a piece of paper, a workplace, a boss, a culture, a government - you are lied to about freedom. Freedom is a kind of con game in this world; it's held in front of your eyes as a tease while you're chained to a bank. So the solution to this situation is to play the game while knowing it's a game, so one day you may leave it - or even change it. That's like being awake while asleep in a dream; it's a tremendous advantage. You can wield that knowledge to better your position as you see through the illusions that once had you trapped.

What we are naturally will forever be more glorious than who and what we become linguistically as individual ego's. You really don't comprehend how fascinating you are, do you? It is not of me to write this, but rather for you to intuitively know just how marvellous your being is within this universe. I'm willing to bet that this morning, or tonight, wherever you're based - there lives an unsettling feeling inside your heart. It's probably haunted you for some time. And I'm willing to go further and say it's what brings you here, to reading this book or exploring social media feeds that share philosophical and 'spiritual' content. However, I feel it is a part of my integrity to admit there's only so much to gather here as ingredients for the growth of your soul.

If you are sincere, and I assume you are about this awakening path, then there is an immense amount of it that you must journey alone. These are my words, the voice of my spirit came to me in solitude, during breakdowns in a lonely house at nightfall; but you need yours. You need to speak your truth; to not solely follow and consume, but voice your essence into being, and you will come alive.

Too many people underestimate themselves. They misuse their intelligence; they're misinformed. One main difference between where they are and where they wish they'd be is due to not understanding who they are, and what they're capable of. See, most thoughts generated by the common individual focus on distractions. These diversions influence the being to think primarily of self-image, which relies on locating flaws within their physicality, social status and monetary growth. When this happens, we already see the attention divert from their strengths and into fabricated accomplishments. Those supposed fulfilments are made-up because they're based on an entire societal structure existing purely from the collective imagination of members of that society and implemented with everyday language. As such, the person never gets to reach their potential. Instead, they're focused on the lives of celebrities, global brands and finding value in material that can occupy their mind. It's saddening. Call me naive, but I genuinely think everyone is an intellectual. However, people are afraid to think for themselves and some are just too far deluded and imprisoned by their culture.

Philosophy is my medication, my ego is the patient -
my soul is the therapist. I must communicate with my
soul utilising philosophy if I am to understand my ego
and use it for better. Otherwise, what's the point? Why
live if you're only to bury your mind in the thoughts
of others when there's a blazing universe to
understand and explore; both internally and
externally?

Humans are remarkable; I think we've forgotten that. We are too caught up with defining ourselves by our grades, appearances, our history, employment status and current societal roles - the conscious effort to make light of the fact that each one of us contains the wonderments of the imagination is lost. We drain ourselves of our magic and sell it to the market so that we can fit into some absurd character which doesn't satisfy our happiness. We become miserable, dark, and start treating each other poorly because we don't enjoy who and what we've become. We lose the fascination we had as children to unravel the mystery within; it's killed by adopting monotonous drivel as we shun the voice of our hearts because we fear rejection. We're unsure how our social groups will respond if we were to be more authentic and genuine with ourselves.

One of the most damaging mindsets to be caught within is to think you've failed. To look into the mirror and see yourself as unsuccessful. You may believe that because you don't have what is valued by so many, and you've probably reached an age which should entail certain assets or achievements, according to the norm. But I say it's rubbish - all of it. You are where you are, and that is unquestionably fine as well as reasonable. It is foolish to expect a human to represent or reflect a specific life when we are subjected to chaos beyond imagination. We're all just doing our best with the path laid in front of us; which will inevitably lead us to the same destination regardless of whatever amount of 'success' you have. This is, of course, not to state that you should ignore areas you could work on to benefit your happiness. But just know you don't owe it to anyone or anything to be someone.

Time is not spent. Moments pass and seasons change - but you never had any of it. You think you do; you think you can have something or someone, love or whatever - but all of this will be here long after your existence. You don't own anything in this world; and the sooner we learn that, especially those in power of our collective choices - perhaps we'll treat Mother Nature with more respect for she is not ours to control and command.

I believe it to be more grammatically correct in certain instances to say we 'are' rather than we 'have.' You do not have love; you are love. You transmute yourself into that source when you recognise your very nature within another. It's the humour of life, the paradox; we are more of the internal with what we feel, rather than the outer layer which displays what we 'have.' Yet we identify by the external, the skin and clothing - which is deceiving. Undress the illusion; turn yourself inside out.

I have an unorthodox view of wasting time; I don't believe in it. Even if you have the drive to achieve something important to you, and let's say you partake in an activity that is unrelated to that particular ambition - then that is no waste of time. How can you waste time? Those two words together make no sense. Firstly, time does not exist. Secondly, the abstract notion we have of time indicates we have an infinite amount, not limited. Our biological clock may state otherwise, but where have you been for the past 13.8 billion years in the (observable) universe? Wasting time? No. Wasting time is something they've invented to keep you anxious. However, some of the most precious moments of living are in doing absolutely nothing.

I think death may present the most outlandish, zany, alien-like event an organic creature can have. It will make a psychedelic experience seem mundane. It will be where all memories, dimensions, worlds and realms blend in one giant mash-up accelerating at higher speeds as you witness the happening wide-eyed like the first time you observed a sunrise as a kid. Only this time it will be a sunset of some sort; an end to the suffering you've endured because part of existing is to persevere through all the hardships that ought to of had you killed but didn't for you remained resilient and adaptable. Peace will then be met, as well as warmth like you were no longer watching but rather bathing comfortably in the star that sourced your energy. From there, I smile at the thought we retire the body, and our energy is transmitted within the rays of sunlight to enlighten a new day of life for the living on Earth.

Let me guess you. Often, you're wondering if any of this is real. If existence has some message for you to decode to live for as a form of purpose. So you think deeply. But it's hard; because as social organisms, it's challenging to express these consciousness expanding thoughts when you're surrounded by radio, television, peers, family and friends who only cognitively engage in more pop-cultural interests. That is fine for some parts because it can be entertaining.

But then there's that itch for something more; a longing to have a night shared with a like-minded individual watching space documentaries that proceed to star-gazing beside a fire with soulful conversations which suspend you both astrally. However, you don't. Consequently, and believe me, because this happened to me - it all bottles up. You begin the retreat. Friends become ghosts. The average night out turns into researching esoteric knowledge indoors. You shift your focus towards philosophy, science, spirituality, astronomy. Then you're taken away by the first statement at the beginning of this written piece which was, you're wondering if any of this is real.

Among many who have lost their third eye to countless addictions and luring advertisements, I see you. I can discern your powerful aura from across the planet. You're unique and intuitive; brilliantly gifted but tragically self-critical - I recognise the soul that yearns for another like you. You're not alone. Many share your thirst for intellectual growth and consciousness expansion. Avoid sleeping back into the matrix. Stop it from robbing you of your gift. Pursue knowledge, listen to nature, and trust yourself.

Be careful, spirituality has become a market to sell all sorts of gimmicks. It also seems to be adopting people who feel unnoticed, and who wish to have a sense of belonging and identity for some degree of attention. Therefore, they find refuge in dressing, speaking and acting 'spiritual' as it is an esoteric practice, which will raise eyebrows and give them the satisfaction of recognition. To be known is a popular desire in modern society.

Of course, this is not everyone, and the opinion is solely based on the observation of one man. However, I think it's important to state that spirituality is about communicating with the spirit, not accumulating material or aggrandising the character. I wouldn't recommend deceiving yourself; it's troubling enough as it is to be lied to by others. And to exit from one mental state and into another which views itself to be egoless will surely lead you in circles. Be real, be genuine, be curious - or you may as well not be spiritual but religious.

I'm young, but I feel old. I
feel like I've been here before;
like I've danced under the
light of a million moons and
had my spirit kissed by a
thousand different suns. My
body is here, but I'm from a
different age, another world -
another time. So please
excuse what you've defined as
eccentric behaviour, I'm just
not from here.

People rarely say what they're thinking; their honest thoughts are killed by good reason. You see, a person sleeps with silence rather than inform their spouse they've fallen out of love with them. Consequently, they seek intimacy from another source while continuing a dead relationship. I don't like this, but what is the alternative? Truth hurts the blind, like light to closed eyes; no one enjoys being woken from a dream.
One of my most difficult challenges is my internal conflict of empathy and brutal integrity. I'm sharp and will tell you exactly what I am thinking. However, this attitude can act as a catalyst for pain to surface within the recipient, and therefore, I feel it too. But I don't believe in bottling what I have to express if I am involved. I prefer the real over the dream, and I respect those who show it to me even if it burns my ego or pride, and this is written by a Leo.

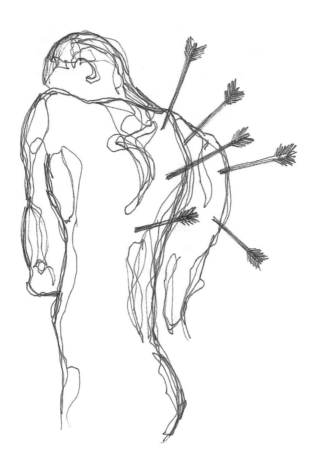

I think it is necessary for your sanity to see the stars. To keep your head up, especially when the world has you held down in the pettiness of the game. We've questioned for many years how we came to be so intelligent, so alert and alive and of course, it will probably be an answer that we will never know. However, I believe a significant factor at play that enhanced our cognition was the sight of space, or more specifically, the ability to look up and see there is more beyond what is present in our immediate surroundings.

Imagine you're located on an isolated island by the ocean as a primitive person with no understanding of foreign lands or what is out there on Earth - and you wonder. You fire the imaginative thoughts sparked by curiosity and endeavour to find out what lies at that edge of the water that seems to predict a giant fall. So you begin to move, collect, build. It's quite daunting - to leave behind your island of known truths and make a fragile boat to go out and explore, but that is the price of growth. This is evolution by the expansion of your perception, which is why sources that influence just that such as psychedelic drugs are outlawed because the last thing you want when attempting to maintain a system (island) as an insecure and fanatic government is to allow your people to explore the edge of the water. Nevertheless, you do this, and you realise how caught up you were in a boxed reality. Keep your head up, your eyes to the stars and beyond as you dare to push the boundaries of modern understanding.

We've lost a significant amount of love for life. Even our very being is a turn-off. A lot of us struggle to look into the mirror without perceiving some atrocious, ugly thing staring right back. And what is this? We abhor existence so immensely that self-loathing isn't enough. I believe the destruction of nature - this animosity we feel towards this planet and what we do is an externalisation of self-hate, a corruption of the collective psyche of humanity projected. It probably began with ego unable to accept itself as a fabrication, so it dominates to simulate a tangible presence in a frequency wave of vibrations and energy that is the universe. The exploit of deforestation to create lifeless structures relates to the everyday individual who strips themselves of their soul in place of the material for a sense of identity. It's an insecure imprint for reassurance of our existence. We're a suicidal species at odds with nature; we're destroying ourselves.

We're strangers to ourselves; that's the tragedy. The youth befall to this misconception of their identity often, as they ruthlessly contour both their bodies and minds to resemble some reputable appearance relative to mainstream culture; while modern education tears through their creative potential. Their lexicon suffers, slang is their primary expression, their consciousness becomes restricted - their reality limited. I've said this before, and I struggle to find an opposing viewpoint which dismisses this thought as foolish, but everyone is gifted and intelligent, we just pretend not to be. We give ourselves over to some model of behaviour as a means to source meaning and truth in dull environments and people. Consider those who sacrifice their sexuality to meet the dominant image circulating culture, as they forfeit their love and energy to maintaining a dead relationship because of the outside judgement. It's a cruel thing to do to yourself, to be someone and somewhere you don't want to be, yet believe you must because it's normal.

As a thought to play with, think about our size in the universe and the odds of returning here; implying that this may be the only human experience you'll ever undergo in this bizarre realm, therefore - make it count. However, not by attempting to mislead yourself into becoming something more than what you are, but the contrary, to understand who you are, which is everything you decide to be when no one, including your ego, is looking.

Avoid the holy (wo)man syndrome. It is the delusion of awakening only to feel superior to others, and therefore feeding an inflated ego, which contradicts the awakening. At the core of our endeavour is the realisation of the underlying unity between us, our environment, our fellow earthlings and all else that exists in this vast, infinite universe we call home. There is no game of hierarchy.

I know of people who have an interest in their higher self; practising their yoga, meditating during their days, but for some - the idea and image of this are far greater than the purpose itself. That is a very damaging trick to play on the mind. The holy (wo)man syndrome, the spiritual ego, whatever you want to call it - can take you on a deceitful trip which ends in a feeling of supremacy accompanied by the belief in unproven information sourcing from pseudoscience. Be honest with this, for I would not advise stating 'facts' wrapped in flowery language and unfamiliar terminology that gives you a sense of self-importance.

What I mean by this self-journey that I write about is to communicate with the mystery. It is a mystery to be alive, it is mind-blowing to be here, and there is knowledge ready to surface by the expansion of your consciousness. Before my investment within myself, I was a depressed, suicidal teenager with an understanding of who I am that went as far as my cultural input. Now, I've opened the mental doors to soul-discovering teachings such as quantum mechanics, philosophy, astronomy and practices of meditation, yoga, and writing. The journey is like the expansion of the universe; your entire human experience is subjected to new areas of thinking you never thought possible.

There is a strong chance that people who feel too much will seek shelter from the world by isolating themselves away as depression eats them alive. But if you can master this state, to endure the ferocious storms of emotions which beat you to your last breath, only for you to return to the outside - you'll experience the very definition of freedom. That is because you have spent your time inwards, unearthing a self through suffering that is much more true to who you are than the character they claimed you to be. And now you can participate as this recently freed individual - thinking for yourself and questioning that which most ignore.

Remember this - we are all on a planet flying through the cosmos, subjected to chaos and strangeness beyond reason. No one has a clue as to what is really happening here. Don't be too hard on yourself; enjoy the ride.

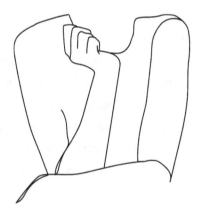

You haven't failed; you're heartbroken, yes, but your life doesn't conclude here. If I may, I want to write this about you, the reader, as I read your story. Of course, logically you will reject such a proposal, but haven't we discovered words transcend all boundaries and exist within us all? Even within a deaf-blind and illiterate person, there is a story that we share. So I feel qualified to say at least something about you, so long as I can tap into myself.

I know you feel let down by the world, by the consistent scrutiny which impregnated the preference to seek solitude, even though the loneliness can sometimes be painful. To not have a lover who speaks with your soul or a companion to explore the wonders of existence with hurts, some nights, sometimes. And it's within those moments you turn on yourself. You question your life choices, your apparent mistakes, your value, and if you're a good human. That can be deadly. It's already too violent with modern society interfering with your mental state, so to have your ego generate such negativity will certainly destroy you.

I know you probably want to make something of yourself too, and the fact it's beginning to seem unlikely is unsettling, or maybe you've already come to terms with that. The idea our lives will be forgotten in a universe too big to deem us important will take even the most famous among us and remind them they are no different from that of a sea worm in the cosmic scale of things. We're all waves in this ocean, no larger nor more significant than the other.

In moments of distress, sit with yourself, and let everything psychologically bleed; the hate, the suicidal thoughts - scream if you must, just ensure you communicate with yourself. Always remember there are beautiful people in the world who understand and are willing to offer their love.

Never let guilt or regret continuously
weigh down your limited days under
the sun. You can do no wrong,
fundamentally. And you can always
make good of yourself if you try; if you
investigate and be truthful about what
you did by enlightening your problems.
Mistakes occur, we're human - we're
biologically made of billions of them.
There'd be none of this if the 'error' of
colliding planets and exploding stars
did not happen. It's a play of energy -
allow yourself to dance to the beat of
vibrations. You're born each moment
anew, so don't feel attached to a self,
event or action that is no more. I think
that is a universal message providing
clarity for organisms subjected to harsh
mental conflicts; that peace can be
attained in the moment. It's only a
matter of accepting the past as it was
and embracing the now as it is - which
is refreshing.

I believe the primary concern for the suicide epidemic should not be within the act but instead in the rejection of its presence. To classify it taboo within our society which secludes the individual into an even smaller box of violent feelings fueled by an urge to break free will only further the self-harm tendencies. The thoughts should be accepted and seen as an expression of sanity, as to live comfortably in a painful world indicates a lack of feeling, which defines a madman. Take away one's addictions, strip them naked of their distractions, isolate them and see if they can withstand the rawness of their mind; because I don't even think the human mind can handle existence. There seems to be some kind of law where once the mind of an organism becomes conscious of itself, it will either attach to an image that it fetishises or attempt to destroy everything. If you doubt this, then acknowledge the circumstances of our world. People take their lives every day; those who don't are either addicted to something or someone and almost all of us are destroying the planet from over-consumption deriving from the need to sustain this projection of oneself.

This is why meditation is fascinating. If you silence the mind and reconnect with your body - it's like a contradictory escape by going in that does not conclude with you no longer living, but rather actually being present. It's paradoxical and quite literally, mind-blowing.

How can the depths of someone's soul be enlightened
if they are unwilling to travel there and confront that
which awaits? No guru will carry the torch for you;
no saviour will pave the way. It's you who must ask
the questions, and it's you who will find the answers.
Do not for one moment think you're not capable,
you're more than intelligent enough, but it's a matter
of removing the shackles you've place upon yourself
that has you defining your limits by your position
within the human game.

I'm not one to think of myself as possessing any remarkable skill or trait; I'm just honest, which, come to think of that, it has kind of become a remarkable trait in today's world, hasn't it? To be raw and truthful with not only others but yourself too.

Introverted does not mean shyness, nor does it imply the tendency to be emotionally reserved. It's feeling depleted of energy within social environments, typically large, and experiencing mental overstimulation by the excessive observing of one's surroundings, which is information overload for an introvert's brain. As an introvert, the internal me is 'out there' with my feelings and thoughts; so it's not to mistake this preferred state as someone who is entirely unengaging. If anything, I greatly involve myself with an individual as I discern hidden meaning within their body language and hear information which shares more about who they are than what they're verbally expressing; and that requires sincere attention and communication. I feel so much within, swelling throughout my body and spirit, that the outside usually becomes too much to bear.

The saddest part about us and our current destructive habits is that it could have been different. It could have been that we prioritised the well-being of each member of society by meeting their essential standards of living rather than fetishise objects and things that have us crushing one another. To accept our position in the cosmos, rather than turn away from ourselves and find salvation in fallacious ideologies that separate, degrade, disempower and limit the incredible mental strength of a human.

No matter your journey, we're all heading the same way.

To my brothers, my fellow men - I see you. Society lies. Misjudgements influence unnecessary pressure that burdens the mind with misconceptions about what we must be and how we should carry ourselves as men. As such, within those beliefs - we have misunderstood man and his nature with the world. The modern male has consequently become disconnected from his internal self, for his apparent pursuits, along with his identity - are thought to lie in the external. Therefore, he must be strong. He must be able to provide, look, walk and talk like a man. There is rarely an effort to develop and communicate what is present within, for we do not believe our emotions to serve many purposes.

The extreme outcome is the soulless creature who has tarnished the beauty of the masculine with meaningless dominance as an expression for the search of himself. We dominate Mother Nature looking for all these ingredients that identify us as the fictitious man. This leaves the sensitive male misplaced because how they intuitively interact and express themselves is not what's expected, and therefore they're confused and lost - which usually leads to suicide. The female counterpart is also negatively affected as they represent the suppressed feminine energy that men are culturally conditioned to withhold, resulting in this distrust and conflict between the two once confronted.

Philosophy

I am no psychologist or expert; these are just
thoughts I've sourced from somewhere with love and
understanding for my brothers as the underlying
message. I believe for the health of men there needs
to be a radical shift in our connection,
communication and trust with our inner self.

I do not like the social stratification of my society, and I cannot find any reason to believe that we're not capable of implementing a socioeconomic structure which dismantles the 'elite' without corrupting something else. It's nonsense that we must have the rich and the poor; this is the attitude of people sick with the belief that money is real, and it should direct us towards a purpose. Look, I'm not for capitalism, communism, socialism, or what have you. I am for novelty, of embracing the fact we share a planet rich in resources, and we are an extraordinarily intelligent species that can do better. I know, the psychology at hand in the dominant culture which influences minds to fetishise material or even status renders such a state of unity almost impossible. But I'm in this machine, working a dead-end job every day to pay bills and I cannot with one ounce of my intellect agree that humans aren't capable of something better. There's no way you can fly a human to the moon while a human starves for food in the gutter without there being an incredibly major fault in the system at hand. People laugh at me for this. Headstrong individuals always tell me that people won't work and no one will do anything if there isn't a motive, an incentive which provides a selfish reward. However, they're entirely overlooking my perspective. I'm suggesting our scientific discoveries inflating common knowledge which has propelled technological advancements does not reflect where we're economically at; it doesn't make sense. I alone cannot answer this, but humanity can.

If you have the love to expand
your mind and the ability to
turn awareness into words for
others to digest, then you will
be seen as a threat by
authorities. Language is the
nuke of modern times.

The absurd thing about humans is that an astonishing universe exciting mystery surrounds and exists within us, but we're unhappy - usually just because of some shallow reason like money. All along we've been in heaven, but we're caught on a psychological hang up that we do not belong here, that we're unworthy.

Money is the god of gods. People and institutions worship this language, this medium, but I distrust money and these unnecessary troubles that most are willing to go through. I wish to live simply and honestly. I do not want your offerings that encourage a consumerist attitude. I do not want your fancy cars nor flashy clothes, your materialistic drugs that keep me enslaved to this game of empty fulfilment. Spare me the misery of a moneyed man deceived by where his happiness rests and enrich me with knowledge. Settle me by nature with wild friends who live to explore this magnificent world and aren't afraid to look at the stars. That's it, that's my treasure. You can have everything else.

It should not be of money or them to tell me who I
am; that would inflame my insanity and my anxiety.
The voice of the crowd speaks only to overwhelm the
individual with doubt - to outcast them as a way to
influence them to conform. How many times have
you silenced your inner-voice which encouraged you
to do what your soul felt pulled towards because you
were afraid of the judgement? You're defined as
someone by them, and if your desire for writing a
book or becoming an actor contradicts the character
you're seen as by the crowd, then you're persuaded to
dismiss the dream and return to 'where you belong.'
That's death, the true means of losing your life.
Because if physicality is almost totally an illusion of
just vibrational energy, then I think your source of
being is within your love and what you loved.

This game will try to hurt you. It will try to break your spirit as a means to own you; so you rely on its support, which does more harm than good. But do not mistake this game for life, or the only possible world. Reality is, after all - the collective agreeance of the perceived which is determined by the limits of our ability to discern information and that's decided by our senses, minds, cultural and linguistic restrictions. It can be changed, as proven throughout history. If one were to alter their consciousness, channel their energy more productively for self-healing rather than slaving to a system, and acknowledge their faults - then a beautiful transformation can occur.

People mistake what they encounter on the outside as solely an external entity rather than a familiar source originating from within; meaning, the choices we make and the environments we create mirrors the depth of our self-understanding. In my opinion, the majority are confused; hence - the pollution, wars, greed, destruction - as we are disconnected from ourselves on a global scale. We don't look as far inside so we cannot see that far outside. Consequently, we are dying from our misconceptions, and that is accelerated by our hatred for what represents growth through change. It's why we attack Mother Nature and strip her naked from her beauty as we do to those among us who embody novelty such as the youth or freethinkers. They represent change, growth, transformation - which is threatening to a rat race.

Sometimes I'm lost in thought. I look out and question the world, life, myself, and it leaves me with this uncanny feeling. It usually progresses to thinking about what it'd be like to no longer be alive because that makes me laugh. There is so much to us and everyone that death seems to be some kind of joke. It just comes in, usually out of nowhere - and strips you of all that you thought you had.

The only somewhat real reason I have found for my existence is to die. Everything else is a sideshow, a play of words distracting me from this liberating truth. Upon realising that, I have come to know how to live.

A heavily introverted empath, a visionary loner, I'm too much of a dreamer for the scientific, too sceptical for the dreamers. A quiet Leo, preferring the shadow over the light of attention, my mind roars with thoughts of grand measure. I'm a paradox; a free thinker caged by the extent of my knowledge. I'm too alive to die, yet fascinated by the phenomenon of death. It is the night sky which fills me with wonder and taste for exploration, though it is within myself which I travel to unravel an even greater mystery. Life is bizarre, ugly, chaotic but beautiful - as are you.

Say what you like, but I think life on Earth may be as potent with beauty and wonder as everything else in the known universe. We can overlook this because we're a part of it, but who's to say we're not one of the rarest events happening in the cosmos - the evolution of organic life? I don't know if it's that ordinary for sentient creatures to arise from the elements of a dead star; only then to teach calculus and run stock markets as we transfer information near the speed of light with a device which fits the palm of our hand. It's just a thought to consider ourselves as fascinating and mysterious as a black hole - if not more.

Philosophy

You're unsure of what is coming so you don't know where
you'll end up. You barely even know where you are now.
Romantic love is beginning to seem like a con; overhyped
by delusional poets because meeting that remarkable
person just feels impossible. The space you're in right now
is you and only you. Each day is repetitive, as is every
face you see. Your reflection is something you loathe as it
evokes everything you know you should confront but
choose to avoid, which is understandable because knowing
yourself is to destroy everything you thought yourself to
be. Worldly affairs are too much right now. The human
game is so overbearing you can taste the dull, colourless
thing that it is. You want to be settled somewhere in
nature, in a small home, with books and music to
accompany you until your final days. You often think of
what it would be like to be dead; the state fascinates you.
Sometimes you consider it; I know you do - but
somewhere within there's a voice telling you otherwise.

Not because of your morals or some belief or value or fear
or whatever; no, it's because deep in the depths of your
soul you question where else is there to be if not here? Yet
here is indefinable. Where exactly are we? It's like we've
been left behind, forgotten, neglected by a truth out of our
cognitive reach. Therefore, spirituality intrigues you as a
means to find answers. However, mainstream sources of
information related to this area of interest involve some of
the most lost people spreading ideas they've adopted for
comfort; to feel self-important by being alternative.
Navigating it will tear your analytical and shrewd mind

apart as you see past the gimmicks. Consequently, spirituality is something you'll frequently venture alone. You will sit in darkness, letting everything wash over you; the weight of your history drawing forth memories to pressure your mind as it deals with silence.

I don't know where I'm heading with these words, or what made me write this, I guess I'm sourcing some insight for those who read this and relate to it to know that I understand you.

Quietly now, remember who you are. Those supposed attainments numerous individuals share via social media should not disrupt how you see yourself. Your path is different, remember that. Silence the doubt by knowing your truth, which is not for me to give nor for others to have; because deep down you already feel it and it's yours. You know more than I do about yourself, but focusing on the lives of others will influence you to believe you don't. It may not be met this year, but one day soon it will become apparent that all of your miseries contributed to the birth of something too special for words. That's why you can feel it but are confused when you attempt to make sense of the feeling by thinking; which that transforms into overthinking and is intensified once self-judgment is involved by observing the growth and pathways of other people. You're not them; you're you - remember that. How simple but tragic amid ego-inflated influencers do we seem to forget the uniqueness of ourselves.

It may be that by the end of your time, the people you met, the ones you loved and the skin you thought was yours will fade away like the credits to an immersive movie screening your life. Only for you to then wake up, brush your worries away and move onto the next.

Spirituality concerns the practices I've implemented regarding the unspeakable. I don't like spiritual talk; it's too challenging to navigate the flowery language. Often, you don't know what you're being sold by people who don't know what they're preaching. I source my insight directly from my soul. That is not to mislead you; I'm open-minded because I'm aware of my stupidity, but each of us grows here knowing everything there is to understand about spirituality. It's a matter of remembrance. You know what this is all about, even if it takes you a while at first, you'll see yourself in another being. You know very well you're going to be okay too because there's nothing to lose. Your soul is all around you. This body is like clothing. All of us are dressed with matter, appearing to be these distinct shapes and colours, but it's not too challenging to see through this and remember.

If I have yet to do so in this book, I want to welcome you, possibly for the first time, to exist without the confinements of human-made fallacies. To awaken from your cultured perception, and to acknowledge your presence in a universe oozing with possibility and strangeness. Reality as we know it isn't fundamental. It is not the be all and is open to deconstructing and reconstructing if any perceiver is willing to elevate their consciousness. To consider more and consume less. To really go into the art of living, with tremendous passion and a wondrous heart as well as a fertile mind absorbing the most esoteric knowledge a mere mortal can understand, even if it's just for a moment. Be willing to die for what you love, and love while you can. If you suffer, and you will - greet its cruel grasp with curiosity. Know what fuels the pain beneath your skin and mentally cut it open with your intellect; because you are extremely intelligent. You are a stream of consciousness from an unknown source operating a relatively adaptable body in a mystical world filled with enigmatic messages and anomalies. And when it's all too much, find night and a quiet spot by a tree to gaze at the enormity of space. Remind yourself that no one alive has anything over you when the entire planet is subjected to the disorder of the cosmos. That is a method of surrendering your troubles to the universe as it guides your life in this one and the next.

You do not have to look far to realise a conscious shift occurring within the general population. There is a remarkable urge to reconnect with the planet and to each other within a world that is somewhat fuelled by mainstream media pressurising self-image. Although we may not directly see it daily, it is evident by the emergence of social engagements found online and offline that more and more people are beginning to ditch the influences that blindfold their life and instead open their minds to re-evaluating who they are and what existing is all about. And I believe we will not go quietly into our graves unheard and mistreated. We will not be pawns to superficial games, serving as tools to build empires that are inhumane and insensitive to the joys of life. We are the future that inspired our ancestors with purpose when they fronted impossible natural obstacles that ought to have ridden the human race forever.

It can not be that the 21st-century inhabitants are the ones who drop the torch. It is within your chest that the collective heart of our species beats, and I ask of you to take us somewhere wholesome. Revitalise the human spirit that has lost itself to a polluted world of greed and violence. Let our heart beat to soul-uplifting music in awe-inspiring environments filled with wild people hosting far-out minds and ideas. Take humanity to the brink of exploration, undressing the cosmic body with the nerve that we organic creatures can gawk upon untold secrets of space and touch arcane knowledge that was only meant for the gods; as if we dare challenge the threshold of animal-restricted intellectual capabilities. Look after our earthly neighbours - treat them with the respect they deserve. Speak to plants, study science, investigate the psychedelic realm and pursue where you intuitively feel drawn to travel. Beat the heart of our kind with passion and love, with might and curiosity.

Every intelligent person questions if they're stupid. Every opinion or answer they have is squeezed with every ounce of their intellect for truth. Ignorance is unwelcome; no prejudice thought is safe. The unconscious is enlightened; any hidden agenda they have tucked away that dictates their decisions or actions is made known and rectified. Group thinking is repulsive. Wise intellectuals are flexible, unmotivated by gains which strictly contribute to their identity and assure their existence; they do not belong to anything or anyone. You can't buy them; you can't pressure them into agreeing with you by threatening some reputational loss. They are for discussions, the sharing of information to expand awareness. Such people are irreplaceable.

I understand how you feel. After all, although we go about our daily lives playing as some character - underneath those illusive identities we are directly connected with the knowledge that we're human. Do you know what this means? My fundamental position in life is the same as yours, you see? I'm on this roller coaster of a world just like you. And my darkest days have been met by the cruellest nights in bathroom mirrors as I stared at a body I no longer wanted to have as the container of my eternal energy. I fought self-projected demons and battled what cannot be seen, heard or felt.

Meanwhile, this planet flew through space and time in a solar-system way out on the edge of an average galaxy, spinning among others in a cluster of absolute mayhem. However, every morning was kissed by rejuvenation, and each day I was always met by you. Another face, another soul, another universe bottled up inside decaying flesh subjected to the human realm from a perception unknown to mine but still a part of my journey. So know when I say I understand you, I acknowledge what it's like to be alive. Although circumstances may vary from individual to individual in regards to specific events, we still share the qualities and aspects of human experience.

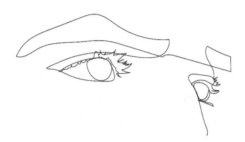

Occasionally I catch a glimpse of my
soul when I'm not looking.

Speak your truths, and never sell yourself to an image. Be critical, sceptical - don't just believe and use terminology that speaks for you, but know what you are thinking. That is to 'spell,' to weave your magic rather than be spelled and controlled by cultural influences. Honour science, philosophise the unknown, respect nature, observe yourself - and you will experience the mystical. Too many people are lost to hype causing them to be persuaded by deceptive manipulators that have marketed philosophy and spirituality. Recognise the signs; correct yourself if need be. And if you're tired, finding the thought of eternal rest much more beautiful than the intricacy of human affairs - then reconsider your surroundings before you decide to sleep for eternity. It's a journey - one with an extensive history that can be tracked like footprints in the snow when you become conscious of the synchronicity. You may discover meaning there, enough to find value again in the living.

It's an odd experience to encounter an old friend,
especially if you are on this path of self-exploration.
It's like you've traversed unspeakable lands and
visited unimaginable worlds, so to speak where you
left off as if you've never changed is impossible.
There's an empty silence that is contradictory for it
is filled with infinite thoughts you're unable to share
because simply put - the person just wouldn't
understand.

Keep the explorative mind you had for knowledge as a kid alive; never settle for some final view of the world. The imagination is the elixir of freedom, and every attempt by authorities to reduce its power is an attack on the human experience. It's a war on consciousness, and if it isn't then I am baffled by the lack of support in our educational system and the general public interest of what it means to be alive. Consider your situation; an adaptive organism loaded with incredible mental strengths cannot be subjected to the limitations of identity-restrictive concepts such as nationality, race or a grade on a piece of paper that dictates your intelligence and status. That's a very small minded perspective that doesn't hold up in regards to your anatomy, origin, potential and magic-like abilities such as dreaming. We can do so much more for ourselves, each other and this dying planet if we take a moment to appreciate the art of philosophy and reflect upon our motives which signifies an act of raising our consciousness. Regain your life, take back your mind and be willing to explore regions of deep-thought and meditative states that seem to be frowned upon by modern governments and societies.

It is a damn shame we need reminding of who we are not, which is everything they claim us to be; for we are far greater than that - and that's what they're afraid of us knowing.

Know yourself; that is what they are afraid of. Know who you are, and you will never be under their control. Treasure your ability to process information as the most intellectually advanced organism on planet Earth and be courageous enough to learn what most ignore. And if you make errors along the way, do not insult yourself - just observe the confusion, discover the correction and grow. Our ability to create what is known as the mistake provides us with the possibility to grasp and formulate an answer.

We must stop treating this world as stock on the market and instead appreciate it as an artwork on a canvas to be admired and explored.

There are many layers to what you see before you, within any human. No matter their appearance, shape, colour, status or whereabouts - all glean the forces beyond the ordinary and have parts of themselves that exist elsewhere.

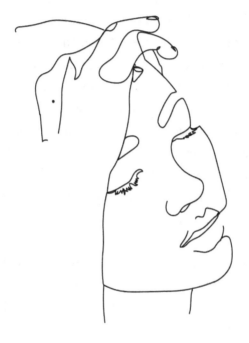

Before the eternal night, remember yourself. Before your
heart sleeps the beat and your eyes shut the dream,
remember yourself. Not the 'I.' Let I die. Let it disintegrate
and echo millions of thoughts that reflected a false identity.
Like glass from a mirror shattering an image into tiny
fragments of what it had believed to capture as the whole
but failed to do so, as the real body still exists after the
breaking of a mirror. Remember yourself. Hear your voice
in the breeze that sound the trees of age, and feel your body
pour through your hands when you hold the water of a river.
Find your eyes scattered in the night sky, beyond what the
furthest sight your optical jewels can visually discern and
know your flesh spans across Earth in many forms of
organic mixtures - even if your current body sleeps tonight
in some lonely city. Remember who you are; that's it. Before
you were born, before the birth of any human, before the
beginning of this decade.

If you dare to travel there, beyond the horizon of self, you
will do so alone. Be wary of yourself. You will be your hero
and your beast. Only you will be able to take away the
energy you're feeling and silence the deep-thoughts you're
exploring, do not let that happen; embrace the solitude. I am
but a whisper in the wind, an echo of a man, a footprint of a
forgotten person. These words are not mine; you own them
now. Make of them what you will, because from here on out,
it's you and only you. If you dare to travel there, beyond the
horizon of self - you will do so alone. All of the world and
their judgmental eyes will intensify upon your ascent, but
how much power you give them is your decision. Just as

how much significance you give this passage is your decision; it's all about you. And considering that is the case, be willing to know who you are or be forever shadowed by the figures of others as you return to your couch and TV, slumped in a mould of repeated failures. If you do dare, and you will if you're sincere about yourself, then give it your all or forget about it.

As you sink your consciousness into the cosmos and intoxicate your mind on its ichor, you'll open up communicative pathways for you to enrich your soul on the quintessence of the universe. Thus, allowing your existence to be enlightened by the source that flows within and all around you. This is achievable if you deconstruct your mind of the linguistic programming that has you systematised to a particular race, nation, culture and society - fundamentally designing some sort of illusion known to you as your reality. And instead, 'turn yourself inside out' so to say, by looking within and discovering the natural happening that you are, which is in harmonious sync with everyone and everything else. Egoless, in that moment, you will intuitively understand who you are, and what your purpose is in your cosmic flash as a human. Re-emerging from the universe pool, and returning to human affairs, soaked from the heavens you will drip with cosmic energy that modern society will reject, as you will be seen as alien, weird, strange - and that is beautiful; for you will embody qualities that will change the world.

Consider this, you are living in a field of information. Imagine TV static, waves of data encompassing your perception. The body you effortlessly grow is an organic instrument or suit which fine-tunes itself into the field and consequently allows the human experience. You receive, transmute and project this information according to what you have sensed or believed as truth; which is what we collectively define as reality. It is, therefore, of the utmost importance that we are wide-awake of our current limitations so that we may one day surpass them. If you settle for a belief, then you will be left there. The doors of possibility will close, and you will live the remainder of your human happening as such until death grants you the release to rejoin the field as the field before washing back up in it as another form of life.

In regards to this thought-practice, know the words you use and what is yet to be worded. Otherwise, life is like being stuck inside a prison made of language without the ability to grow as you are controlled by the input of others. For example, look at your phone in your hand, and acknowledge the inner-world (apps, profiles, text, images.) Imagine being inside the screen, born within there and locked to the current slang, trends, news and shared discoveries. But outside the screen, there is an entire physical universe. That is what I'm urging for you to break free from.

Somewhere in this world rests a person who doesn't say much, though they have a lot to say. They paradoxically know what is real, what is true, which is that certainty in any truth disregards the truth there is no certainty in anything. Nothing is known; all before us is an elaborate hallucination of drugged up animals holding together a reality through the web of linguistics, as even our existence is in doubt. They don't say much, because who can when your thoughts are out of place? It's the result of a person who has finally found themselves after years of searching; an act of rebellion against the world-wide establishments hindering independent thought as a means to control and disempower. So there they are, unbeknown to the world but rich with novelty and depth.

The weather has changed. I can feel it again - the archaic, arcane source pool beneath my feet and surge throughout my body. What you're about to read as your eyes meet every word are thoughts I occasionally withhold. It's outlandish, and history shows our dislike for people who represent the bizarre. We are a species that seems to hate what is evident. We hide, we run; we formulate truths that behold nothing but lies. For a long time, my mind has crossed back and forth from our illusion and to it. It as in what you deep down know, but refuse to admit.

Sit with me for a moment as we're not truly separated, so there is no need to continue the lie that I am not there, especially considering everything you read of me is a part of you inscribing me into your complex cognition until we're one. Take note, that was a slight allusion to what I am hoping to express. Now, as we are, observe what is near you. Your phone? Good. What holds it? Your hand? Great. And where are you? Home? Fine. An electronic device no taller than a dollar bill contains a bodiless library as vast as all the physical libraries combined with billions of humans mindfully roaming within, and it rests in the palm of a sentient organism. Excellent. Now, together, let's leave this space. Who's outside? Family? Friends? Neighbours? Another human hosting a universe with potent creativity swelling inside a bag of skin that breathes intricate systems of cellular activity and neurological networks. Grand. How about we walk forward on to the grass? Our feet are touching individual hairs of Earth. We stand, rooted in the body of a planet swirling in a galaxy travelling 1.3 million miles per hour. The "it" I refer to is precisely this. Life is a work of sorcery, and you're the wizard suspended in space pulling it all together.

A few years ago, when I was mentally unwell from crippling depression and anxiety that disheartened my soul, I would lay every night outside surveying the stars - hoping to see something extraordinary. I wanted to be taken away; I wanted to be abducted by some space travelling entity.

It was in reflection of that wish that provided me with a powerful epiphany as I laid in my garden one night. You see, I thought I hated life but in actuality - I just didn't want to be within a world that made me feel so torn and trivial. I wanted to be elsewhere, but the only elsewhere I believed existed at the time was dead. However, due to the support of philosophy and spiritual development, I now understand the world I felt so shackled to is just an insignificant illusion that misleads the collective and that there is much more to our being and this universe than one can imagine. You just have to unlock the mental doors through self-awareness practices such as meditation or yoga and leave behind the places and sometimes people you've outgrown.

Always have time for yourself, my empathetic friend.
Your sensitive soul has you meeting the needs of others at
the sacrifice of your self-care; it is not wise of you to
continue this way. Your desire to better the world around
you is exemplary; you've always had that aura, which I
love you for that. Nevertheless, my words heed the future
breakdown that is unavoidable unless you take that soul-
empowering energy radiating throughout your body and
direct it towards the invaluable person who needs it most
right now - you.

Most of what I write is unreadable,
for the meaning lives in a different
era of thinking. Heck, a lot of what I
am does not belong in this generation
for my peers do not speak my
language or share my passion for
meeting the unspeakable. I feel so
alien sometimes, some days. If you
understand me, you're the minority,
the rare gems of the world; for I
write to a different age, to a different
kind of eyes - to people of deep-
thought with appetites for universal
knowledge. I write to spirits of love,
but not the love that is commonly
thrown around by aspiring poets and
overly enthused young couples, but
the kind that transcends time and all
possible reason that an immature
sentient organism such as myself
could grasp in such a short lifespan. I
write to them, and in return, they gift
me the warmth of knowing I am not
alone - that others exist in this
mysterious world who think and feel
just as I do. The key is to be yourself
so you can be found.

Remember, there are others like you - wandering
alone in this damaged world. I can sense their
energy in the ether. They think like you. They see
through the illusions and are daring enough to
remain curious about existence. Like you, they
know there's more to being alive than the human
game; which is why you'll often notice them
stargazing, creating magic, philosophising,
dreaming, loving and treating all forms of life with
respect. Sadly, most will be alone. Modern society
rejects such dreamers. Thus, you must search. But
not in an ordinary way, for as stated, who you're
looking for are not ordinary; neither are you. And
you will not find them with just your eyes; not with
only the two that sit either side of your nose
anyways. You must use the other to find the others -
your third eye. And as you search, be aware of your
environments. Just because the surroundings may be
congested with individuals who seem to be
disinterested in challenging their reality, an 'other'
may await amidst the crowd, trying to ignore their
expansive mind by drowning it with attempts of
fitting in. Speak to them. Create something
beautiful. People who change themselves are
capable of changing the world.

Be human, please. See me as yourself; I feel, I bleed, I cry and have fears. I ask of you to remove your mask and be authentic, be real with our connection. You and I, and all of humanity for that matter are way out in this universe, in a modest solar-system on a small planet, let's not further our difficulties with lies and manipulations. These shallow games that separate our worlds and cause us to fight each other are unnecessary. Please, sit with me - I know you feel the same. We're going to die; there's no denying that. But as we live, let us savour the moment while we have it, in harmony and balance. We have our supposed differences, but all I ask in this moment is that we don't, that we quiet our minds and appreciate the beauty of today.

Just because you don't have a degree or a strong educational upbringing does not mean you have nothing to contribute to a field of study which piques your interest.

Your occupation or your financial status does not indicate your worth or abilities. You are not your job, and should never feel judged by the most common question asked when greeting someone new or familiar, which is "what do you do for work?" As if the surreal elements that construct the framework of your space-exploring mind which harnesses mental power unlike anything else we know of in this entire universe can be instantly understood and met by how you make money. It doesn't work like that. I am a postal delivery officer. By day I deliver letters and packages, yet come evening - my mind roams the depths of philosophical reflection to write this book. Meet me by day, and I doubt you'd know where I am by night.

From here, pledge that you will honour yourself. That you will confront that beast sleeping in the core of your heart, and with might allied by conscious power, you shall defeat any internal threat that dares oppose your dreams. No thought that arises to bring you down with insecurity will prevail. No attitude that slumps you further into the couch of complacency and laziness will determine your ends. This is your life. This is your dream. You wield the force of the human spirit and a body of incredible resilience. Your ancestors did not fail you when challenged by the harsh wilderness and traversing foreign lands that evoked immense fear; they pressed on and fought with the unmatched determination and energy that continues to flow on within the very essence of your existence. You host every ingredient and tool needed to take you up that towering mountain of mental difficulties that has you stumbling through depressive periods. This is it. This is the message you've sensed for too long of a time; make the change, go forward. You are at the forefront of human evolution, and nothing of this world can drown you into submission other than yourself.

As each day goes by, and I get that little bit older -
I'm becoming more familiar with the process of
discerning meaning by what is yet to come. What I
mean by this is, each present experience that hosts
either a small change or a great disturbance in your
life has a message that cannot immediately be
understood; there's usually an epiphany that greets
you further down the track as you tie all the events
together. A moment of, "Ah, all that I felt, all those
nights of pain and confusion, I see now." When you
understand that, the lesson is not to act with
immaturity from uncertainty the next time you face a
disturbance, but to take your time; sit with your
emotions.

Be a student to your happening, watch for signs, and
be prepared for whatever life has to teach you when it
comes time. I departed from someone I dearly loved
not long ago. I'm only now understanding the
meaning. Life kind of flows backwards like that; it all
sources from something ahead in time that we cannot
see.

Mostly, the mental perseverance with life is based on how much we believe we're real. It's probably part of why we seek attention, to be reassured we matter, that we're made of matter, definite, here - as opposed to fundamentally existing as an enigmatic force with no true substance, beginning or end. If you lose touch with who you believe yourself to be and are uncomfortable with your higher-self, depression will influence suicidal thoughts, and it intensifies for those who heavily rely on validation and meaning from external sources. I considered this when I read a question that asked what makes me feel; which, after enough thought - my answer was the idea that I'm real. I know I'm no more than hydrogen, carbon, nitrogen, oxygen, protons, neutrons, electrons, quarks, words - nothing. Though, my belief in myself that I'm human, able to touch and emotionally respond to my environment enacts as a catalyst to source feelings from music, others, and all else that surrounds me.

Your Gods and theories are words.
Furthermore, language cultivates,
manipulates, deludes, creates, and sculpts
minds to produce truths. When necessary for
recovery - remove language; do not speak,
do not think which is to deprogram yourself
and you are left without an ego; you are in a
state of enlightenment. When you can see
through the world of words, you may then be
able to wield the most influential instrument
with some form of control instead of being
labelled, ridiculed, degraded and subjected
to the potency of language. You'll use it to
empower yourself as well as others, and
influence the world which is to manipulate
reality because you broke through. The
human realm is coded, learn that.

It's still, and you're alone. The time of day is unknown; your body feels as if it's levitating in space, void of the human affairs that gravitate you away from what is real. No one is here to pull you into their fantasy. You are what you are and who you were before you became someone. There's no need to suffer here; no need to burden your mind. This is the environment between the stars, where the basis of nothing succeeds what something is. There is no boss here - no bank breathing down your neck or social pressure from damaging relationships. If there were a way to relate your position that is ageless and infinite to a common word, it would be the interval of death - a brief reunion with the source of existence. How do you feel?

Use this thought experiment, a form of meditation through the power of the imagination as a means to destress your body from what can occasionally be an overwhelming world.

There is a voice, a communicator of profound knowledge in each of us. As a writer, I occasionally feel cryptic messages within myself that are not intended just for me, but for others too.

He's unfit for modern culture. A lover of books, art
enthusiast, a male poet doesn't cut it in conversations
where people his age gather. If anything, he's mocked.
A true man from his environment is to drink alcohol
and slur nonsense after a day of gritty work with the
boys; he can't dine with the philosophy kings, drink
the ichor of gods and speak about untouchable realms
of consciousness. That's no man. So there he is,
outcasted and alone, a forgotten fool.
Know I'm with you, my fellow men.

Understand me; I am of this Earth but not
of this world. I am in this time but belong
to a different age. I do not wish to have
these things that so many spend energy to
attain. I live a simple life; I do not seek
anything exotic in the physical - although I
am in search of the extraordinary that
resides within us all. I am fascinated by
nature, by you and your complexity - truly.
I don't fit that well within modern society; I
don't have many friends, but I know there
are brilliant minds out there waiting to be
found and heard. My words echo their
voices; their faces fill my dreams, and I
feel their presence when I close my eyes
only to open my third.

These days, I am more alone than usual,
but more complete than I've ever felt - and
I'm delighted by that. I'd rather this as
opposed to spending my days pretending to
be someone I don't enjoy, only to entertain
myself with popular outings I don't even
want to be at to see people who have zero
interest in my true thoughts or well-being. I
much prefer it like this, although it's not
perfect - at least it's real.

Your misunderstanding of me is not something uncommon to me. I'm hard to capture, especially with words and labels. So every time you attempt to define me, you see, I know you're entirely overlooking everything I am. I don't fit anywhere. The 'spiritual' don't want me; I'm too psychologically equipped with a shrewd mind that burns through pretenders. The scientific I respect, but even scientist can have psychosis, and science collapses in on itself under the realisation that it depends on mentally deranged organisms fueled by irrational emotions. We can't escape this; there isn't anything objective existing that we could comprehend and understand as it is in its raw state. Therefore, as I said - you misunderstand me, as your perception of who I am reflects something internally within yourself.

Midnight, like a ghost, I roam the hallways of this
empty house, haunting myself I think I've grown
outside of my body; as is the consequence of living
alone with an unbounded mind. I observe what I am,
like a mirror I intend to confront the watcher, the
onlooker, that which is consciousness but never
entirely conscious of itself. It's hidden, deep in the
cracks of existence and every thought I have, my
eternal self and yours too seeps through everything. I
sense it in the corner of my eyes, but the moment I go
to look, it disappears. Just as I attempt to word this, I
fail to capture it all.

My dreams have changed. I'm seeing people I do not
recognise, but conflicting as it may be - they're
familiar. Faces of new, but energies of old, I've met
them before. They say nothing, but tell me
everything. When I attempt to speak to them, only
blank stares greet my mortal voice. I'm unsure if that
is their manner of communicating the message that
who they are is what I once was, for their voices are
now dead, but their presence still lingers buried
within the history of my soul. Or perhaps there are
instrumental people out there I'm bound to meet, and
I'm seeing them now, within my dreams. Either way,
I'm engaged with this; inflamed by the quintessence
of existence my very being pulsates with its strength.
The ordinary is unordinary, the normal is strange, and
we are coated by it all yet pretend not to be. I cannot

help but to want to reveal it for anyone who dares to seek, even if that takes the effort to break words apart and letter them anew for the sake of understanding what exactly we are.

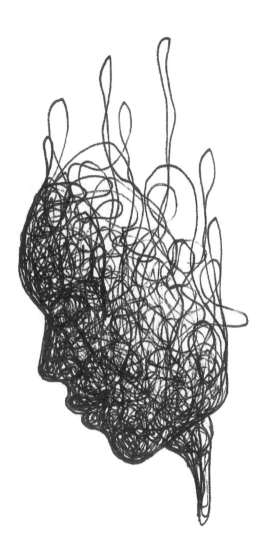

Unless you understand the commoner, empathise with those who suffer, feel the heartbeat of this planet and are comfortable within your skin - what good would money do for you or this world? You'll be lost with your riches; dedicating all of your time to spending your life in search of buying one within a game that sells you nothing but materialistic trash, marketed as soul-enriching treasure, manufactured from greedy corporations for short-lived pleasures. That purchase you're making of creating some image or identity at the expense of your energy so that you can fit in and feel good, it's a trap. Money does not buy happiness. It is beneficial for only those connected with themselves and humanity; otherwise, you'll probably destroy yourself.

We seem to know more about banking, running stock markets, what god to please and which political party to vote for as opposed to the inner chambers of our minds and what makes us happy.

I'm in the mood to undress you of the character you play and reveal the god underneath. I don't care that I haven't met you, I know you have your demons and unsettled history which involves trauma but look, I love you. We're here; we are this masterpiece, a cosmic mystery, energy vibrating so fast we appear to be these physical beings with weird faces and strange limbs, but what we truly are is as remarkable as the most gorgeous of stars. Regret, fear, guilt, you're cleansed of it all as long as you choose to identify your 'mistakes' and be present with the happening, which is to acknowledge the real you. To be human is to suffer, I get it, and it's important to feel that - though there's so much beauty here, within you and all around us. It's pulsating, beating within our lovers, our passions and every day; granting us the opportunity to marvel in awe. It's a work of art, incredible. You are infinitely greater than anything I can write.

Too many knowers in this world. Too
many insecure people seeking to
establish themselves as important.

It's an enormous universe, and
you happen to think you know
all of the answers to it? With
words, a creation of humankind
to guide you along with your
limited biological senses, you are
willing to throw yourself to an
ideology which so effortlessly
explains it all? An ocean is more
than just water.

Breathe. Focus. That is the fundamental of life; the in, and the out. You are no superhero. You don't have to be a leader, no guru, no master, no saviour, no red cape to save the day. Your true form is wordless. You are the middle of the night, a solar eclipse, a distant rumble of thunder, a drop of rain, an explosion and the aftermath. Coming and going like waves - you are it. And the moment you step into it, you'll free yourself like a word revisiting its form as ink before it was sculpted; before a drop of cosmic ichor fell into the hands of control freaks and became fooled by their motives, their games. You know who I speak of - liars, preachers of delusion that have been led astray from the art of living, because narcissistic desires and petty rewards absorbed everything they were. Breathe. Let them fade away along with yesterday. You are here, breathing, alive - and there is a tremendous amount of enjoyment to experience in just that.

What is real? Whatever you want to believe; it will be as real as you are. But I assume we mean what is truly there as an independent source originating from a substance undeniably legitimate in every sense of the word. Something tangible, self-sustaining, unaffected by the perception or awareness of another. Some would argue they are real. Though when you consider not only are we more space than anything else, that our physicality isn't even that physical at all - and psychologically our identity is dependent on the web of linguistics, which implies its origin is a fabrication, I'm not too sure about how real we are. And if we're not, then how can we define what is? The only difference between this world and when I'm dreaming is that I'm consciously here right now. See, I cannot remember my dream just as when I'm dreaming I cannot remember this world. And as soon as I consciously remember I'm pulled back here, like when I become unconscious, I enter a dream. What is real is nothing.

Nothingness is self-sustaining and unaffected by anything external. Everything else seems more like a hallucination arising from the void. But this is a significant contradiction, downright mind-bending and seemingly absurd as we're concluding that what is non-existent is real. Nevertheless, I don't think there is an answer to this question; we don't know.

*When I speak of meaning elsewhere in this book, regarding there being some kind of purpose, it is not to confuse the fundamental context of what I am addressing here.

I know you're in a position of uncertainty. Your job, your friends, your life - all are becoming a blur; you're awakening. Your mind is adjusting to a new perception like emerging from a darkened environment as your vision attempts to adapt to the delicate rays of sunlight. Loneliness will be experienced. Suicidal thoughts may roam the hallways of your mentality as buried insecurities surface for you will scrutinise every aspect of what makes you real. Relationships will end; however, something new will arise. Something much more fulfilling than the shallow space you once believed was life. When it becomes clear, and it will do trust me, then all the suffering will be seen as nothing more than the bittersweet blessings of a consciousness-expanding transformation.

If you're on a spiritual path, be wary of gurus. Stay clear of business-people attempting to profit from your effort to know yourself better. Don't be captivated by the image, and have your path sold on the market with materialistic symbols and goods. If you're lost, you may feel urged to attain an identity that will give you a safe reason to believe your character is real; don't swap an ego to be controlled by another ego - keep a clear mind. Exercise knowledge with a curious spirit, fall in love with feeding your intellect. The world is your domain of experience, so why give up your fleeting moment of life to the control of others?

This is not to say to live alone and be utterly independent. Instead, I am encouraging you to assess your immediate surroundings and have a higher-awareness of your intake of reality as well as your output. If you wish to partake in popular fashion relative to your interests, by all means, that is wonderful; so long as you know it's an act and that soon you'll awaken from this evanescent dream learning so much about what it means to be alive and human.

I've learned to live with less noise. To live with fewer distractions that would hijack my mentality and spoil the human experience. That has cost me friendships, although it was necessary. It was imperative to have those nights where I stood before myself in my bathroom, fogged mirrors, showering the past, bearing my pain upon my naked skin with no noise from the outside to take my attention away. It was only me, staring into my eyes wondering who's looking. No soundwaves were carrying judgemental thoughts from a bunch of nobodies. I was vibing, communicating with the unspeakable. Forty-square feet turned into a space expedition, journeying through subterranean parts of my mind it was self-revolutionary. That period of time I hold dearly within my heart and recommend all to experience such a connection with oneself.

Remember, by the end of this your body will begin to diminish. You will lose the image you've come to identify as you and be left with only the reflection of worn-out-matter, having experienced so much. Whether you will lose the non-physical part of yourself is another question.

The ego will not be taken from you for it never existed to begin with; that will drift away like an echo of a forgotten person as if they were never there. But what of the mind? Consciousness? Intuition? What of the energy emanating from the mysterious source which has attracted synchronicity related events into your life and provided you with insight beyond linguistic form? One universal thought common in the uncommon thinker is "have you been here before?" The "you" is usually not directed at the identifying factors recently listed, but something much more arcane and ancient. And by here, I don't necessarily mean human or as any organism on planet Earth, but alive somewhere, sometime, out there as something. My god, that's strange; imagining yourself as another creature with a whole other realm of laws to worry about. If you entertain this possibility, and I think it hosts the most sound reasoning for we know ourselves, let alone our planet to be but a freckle on the face of the cosmos - then why do you take seriously the limitations put upon you by insecure establishments and people?

Lack of trust in yourself disputes your existence.

Philosophy

Amidst the current chaos of our world, I want to divert your attention towards the stars. Life here doesn't seem so salient, now does it? There's an implication from the enormity and strangeness which suggests there's more to existence than our game; there's a hint of magic underlying this happening. Within yourself too flows a fundamental source existing outside the domain of language, and what I think to be true, outside of your body as well.

We estimate our observable universe to be over thirteen-billion years old; your lifespan is a mere eighty years. To fear is futile, for we do not need to fight what is unknown; what we cognitively cannot make sense of should not frighten our perishable lives. Long before us, billions of people have come and gone. Beautiful individuals, ambitious minds, they are now no more, but perhaps they are something else, somewhere else. What frightened them never served a fundamental purpose, death washed over and liberated all concerns, providing the possibility for us to exist.

As of now, we're travelling through space. No one knows why; no one knows where we are heading or how we got here - though I would suggest enjoying the view rather than feeling afraid of losing it all.

Most thoughts are no longer produced but rather downloaded from social media platforms and major news outlets. Every bit of information you receive, I urge you to play with, including what's in this book. Don't just read but think, re-read and think again. Otherwise, you're just allowing yourself to be played.

It's dark for you right now because you're trying to remain in the light. Too much light eventually blinds you. Embrace your shadow, and you will see. You will see yourself, possibly for the first time - and no longer will you have to suffer the egotistical illness of perfection. Look around you, and within. There are many doors which unlock new pathways for your learning and growth, but some await in depths unreachable by ordinary conscious thought. Try meditation in absolute silence hours before sunrise. When the night is heavy, and the world sleeps, there is an opportunity to access another state of you; a raw, intense, and profound self. There, not only physically in darkness but mentally engulfed by it - a part of you will surface. Such reflection entails greater knowledge of who you are and what you need right now.

As a side note, you know why so many depressed people commit suicide? Because we've been trained to neglect such emotions and thoughts, which is to isolate a part of one's self. Therefore it grows like a tumour, gnawing at the individual's conscious mind until it's too much. The shadow overloads the light. A lot of people would feel less depressed and suicidal if they understood they are allowed to feel depressed and suicidal. That they can seek answers about themselves by vibing with such a state. I grew to what I am today through the welcoming of this.

The deep critical thinker has become the
misfit of the world - this is not a
coincidence. To maintain order and
control you must isolate the intellectual,
the sage, the philosopher - the savant
before their ideas awaken people. This
will cause a mental implosion from lack
of thought-stimulating conversations and
interactions with others, which will lead
to their demise. That is one of the greatest
tragedies of our time - the unwelcome
thinker whose brilliance will never be
known. You are not alone.

I once had this idea of understanding life as something to be remembered. We speak of being present, which enlightens you to a stage of almost not existing - because you're never caught in the past which is where everything and everyone lives. Hence why during that experience of letting go and wholeheartedly living in the now you become egoless (for the ego is subjected to memory,) and you feel a sense of heaviness removed from your energy until your experience shifts from mental projection into sensory appreciation.

So the world dissolves, along with our identity - because both were tangible solely on our ability to withdraw information from what we cognitively processed and stored. Life as we know it is to be remembered. However, another world is born, or shall we say received when one is no longer fixated on the past. Another life after death perhaps?

Aside from this, I wanted to propose a deep thought for you to think about relative to this topic of memory. Have you ever wondered how nature exists? How life from the beginning of time flawlessly operates as if it has before? Cells, bacteria, the formation of stars and galaxies - all of it knows what to do. Maybe it has existed, many times. Perhaps you have too, and the universe is in a continuous loop of on and off, which may explain those extremely unusual memory-related feelings such as nostalgia, of knowing someone before you meet them. And the ancient database of memory from all these repeated lives you've lived is what we access when we trust our intuition. Intuition is the storage of countless lives. If you don't trust it, you're bound to repeat the mistakes you've made before. Lastly, possibly this entails a meaning to life, which is not to fulfil your destiny you've been doomed to die and relive but to awaken a new one.

As another thought, I don't think our destiny is just to reproduce and stir up some chaos. I believe there to be a deeper meaning to the birth of an organism such as a human. And with a particular perspective, you can come to a very odd thought about life as we know it - and our purpose as a species. Firstly, we have to take Earth as conscious, as in, she has some way of producing change with intention and does have a grand form of awareness unknown to us, even though we may contribute to it.

Secondly, the nature of the will to survive that is evident across species has to be applied to planets, solar systems and galaxies. Meaning, just like us - the giants of space are conscious of their death, and desire to prolong their lives.

Lastly, organisms are to planets what technology is to humans; specifically regarding technology being the extensions of our bodies and awareness. With all this in mind, is it possible that nature which is the mind of Earth - has spent the last hundreds of thousands of years prepping a species to host the abilities and attributes to explore space? To leave the dying star as a means for the lineage of Earth to continue elsewhere in the Milky Way galaxy? We are like a concoction of all that is capable here with the energy and the size or our sun, and the position of our planet - all the plausible ingredients have been poured into the development of us. Therefore, our destiny is to preserve life, look after ourselves and the planet - while we give everything to the idea of traversing space and eventually journeying interstellar.

Any form of information you assimilate does not
rest solely in the external for eternity in one true
state. Once discerned, it will transmute relative to
the cognition of the receiver after processing
through numerous psychological factors, both
unconsciously and consciously. It will coalesce
and be projected forth as knowledge. We're
involved with information, so all truth is
contaminated with our touch, questioning the
authenticity of it.

What I know to be true, and what is actually true, are
probably two entirely different matters.

Let's say you were certain to die tomorrow. That as the clock strikes midnight and the new day begins you will cease to be. What dies with you? What ideas or possibilities will never take form because you gave them no life? No chance due to fear of failure? I am not a motivational speaker, I am a philosopher, and I am only that because you contain depth which sparks my curiosity to question. So as I look at you, I see possibility; I see ideas which I want to feed light. I want you to write that book, create that artwork, produce that song, conquer that mountain, sit by that river and have a moment of oneness with the universe because you represent my idea of brilliantly gifted humans giving all that they are to make the world a little more colourful; a little less sufferable for future generations.

Take in as much as you desire, while you can. But do not try to grasp the moment; if anything, that will make you lose a significant amount of experience. Just be. Breathe. What is not held but felt is real. Hence why love exists long after death but the body does not. You are true if you are here, in sync with your surroundings without prejudice thought that filters what is sensed. You never know the last time you will see a place or person. This is not to cause fright or encourage your anxiety to influence you to go out and do as many things as possible, quite the contrary. It is to remind you that this very second, where you are under the sun is the only place to be, and never again will there be another time like it; so there is no need to try and accomplish everything.

We're all in a hurry to be
anywhere aside from here.
Consequently, we're nowhere, for
we're never there; forever existing
ahead of ourselves we lose touch
of ourselves. It's no wonder so
many feel lost. From a young age,
we're taught to be someone or
somewhere, as opposed to just
being.

Everything you do, and everything you don't may be without profound meaning, but it is not without effect. Every breath, every conversation, every decision and action of yours is the consequence of a ripple that began billions of years ago and will continue to catalyse the surreal experience that is existence for aeons to come. If anything, you can see this all as one grand ripple; as in, the very happening that is the stars is also you.

That longing you have for what is too mysterious for words, I sense it also. I chase it to be honest. I know that sounds absurd, how can an individual balance the conventional lifestyle of displaying a front, an ego which pleases surrounding social relationships such as friends and family, yet dines with the philosophy kings at night in their bedroom? Who engages with esoteric knowledge, informing themselves of the world beyond our world? And I don't mean just the expansive thoughts of questioning life after death; I mean the world outside of this illusion - this game.

As you are, as I am, there is more. More people, more organisms, more planets, more solar-systems, more galaxies, and possibly other universes. Even this very dimension is but a curtain hiding even further dimensions. Unbeknown to us, our lack of sensory development may be preventing the realisation that an entity roams our very room but in a broader realm. Like ants are to birds, we are oblivious to anything undetected by our flesh ridden bodies and culturally plagued mind. The skies may be lit with millions of aliens but all we see are the blissful clouds, and through them, at night, the heavenly stars. So what of someone who reflects in such a profound way? I'm unsure. It's still a quiet path I'm travelling, but I'm finding others along the way.

Let me awake like the sun. Let my light illuminate a world shadowed by a mind tormented with lies. Place me among the stars. Place me high up there in the heavens of space surrounded by the company of my kind. Give me the freedom to fly with the galaxies, to spin and weave playgrounds of planets to display my love for you. Allow me to die. Grant my body the fuel of a comet burning a trail of my history for my energy to be spread across the cosmos. Then, let me awake like the sun, once again - as someone or something else way out there.

Philosophy

We're a weird bunch, but we pretend to be normal for
our sanity. We fight for love, which expresses how
little we know of love. Some of our most significant
achievements become our gravest inventions; our
ingenuity is but a blessing and a curse. We became
literate, informed; explorers detached from nature
only to have ourselves lose a sense of who and what
we are. Ego formed, characters developed, a
reasonable decision to fill this void of identity so we
could produce meaning, purpose, a face and image.
Nothing is like us, not that we know of yet - and that's
a part of our tragedy. We're so animal yet godly; so
limited but bursting with potential. Mentally we're in
an unearthly domain of experience, which I don't
believe our exceptional minds can handle the stress
involved with our monkey-bodies, so we turn to
spirituality for comfort and relief; to lift the weight of
being burdened with an alien intellect. The human
encounter is bittersweet, a song of adversity and love;
don't hate yourself for repeatedly falling when you're
trying to get up - this is inevitable for creatures like us.

At the end of all of this, when death returns us to where we once were, causing us to give up pretending to be anything but an apparition of the universe - perhaps before our last breath we will realise how foolish we've been. To fight and not love seems like such a waste of divine energy. Consider yourself and this earthly experience as a playground for the ingredients of dead stars to organically clothe themselves with these bodies that cease to be like a sunset after a gorgeous day. We're momentarily here, a thousand years from now is not that far away, trying to stay alive in our ideologies that delude us is futile. It's over soon, like today; and realising this may remind you of what matters. We are a part of something special - we are exceptional. People have awoken to this, yet others are still pretending.

ACKNOWLEDGEMENTS

If it weren't obvious by now, I've attempted to acknowledge you, the reader. I wrote these words and this book to communicate my soul to inform you that you're not alone; that I too question the nature of this universe and the world we've created. Other than that, it's 'her' that I recognise and hope she sees me too.

Thank you Henriette for your talent, heart and mind. If only we could have sat together to do this. And thank you Olivia and Rhiannon for your input.

Travis J, Sydney, Australia.
*@findtheothers_*

Made in United States
Troutdale, OR
06/13/2024

20527767R00130